Freedom in Christ

Jackie
His love
Perfect love
Heals
3 John 2

"Oh Lord, I am your servant; yes, I am your servant,
born into your household; and you have freed me from my chains."
Psalms 116:16

Sheila Waits

Love Always
Sheila

TNT PUBLISHING

Acknowledgments

I want to thank my children for rearranging their schedules with the grandkids so I could have the time to make this book happen. I want to thank my two sons, Chad and Ryan Waits, for helping me with all the computer technology and Ryan for designing my web page.

I am so grateful for my friend, Keo Lynch, for talking with me in 2009 and leading me back to what I needed most in my life, the Word of God and the baptism of the Holy Spirit. I also want to thank my friend, Pat Patlen, for suggesting I go to the Healing Rooms for prayer. This was where the love of God began to touch my life.

I have so much love, gratitude, and thankfulness in my heart for Janet and Bob Severdia, directors of the Healing Rooms. You embraced me, encouraged me, and poured the love of Jesus on me. I want to thank my pastor, Patricia King. I have spent nearly two years under countless hours of your mentoring. Your life is such a testimony of the love of Jesus, and I have been blessed by it. I would like to thank Prophet Bob Griffin for the prophetic word he gave to me from the Lord for me to write books. It lit a fire. I would also like to thank Charity Bradshaw. I was so touched by her testimony that God stirred what he had inside me to come forth, I am forever grateful. I would also like to give a special thanks to Courtney Artiste of TNT Publishing for helping me to get this book out, even with her own heartbreak and personal trials. I am forever grateful.

I want to thank all of those friends and family members (you know who you are) who have never left my side, who supported me, and stood by me through the hard times and the good.

Most of all I give thanks to my Father God, who never fails me. I owe it all to Him.

Contents

Introduction

G o with me to the beginning of my story to get an idea of how my life began, and then enjoy the journey of how the love of God brought me to a place of freedom.

This is my story of how powerful of a witness I am of the love of God our Father. He never leaves us and never forsakes us, no matter what we do or where we are in our lives.

This book is a written testimony about a little girl who was deceived by a father figure at a very early age. She had no healing, nor did she have anyone to talk to. So, she kept her secret hidden away in darkness in her heart and soul. As she grew up and fell in love and was deceived again, she didn't know what to do. She couldn't understand how love could be so hurtful. When the people you love the most fail you, you develop a false idea of what love truly is. This led to a heart that became broken, shattered, bitter, and full of unforgiveness throughout her life, causing her sickness and disease.

Then Jesus came in like a mighty flood and took away that broken heart and replaced it with His! For no one on this earth can heal a broken heart, broken spirit, or a broken body, only Jesus can. This book is about finding Freedom, Life, Liberty, and Living in the Glory of Jesus Christ.

My prayer is that the power of the Holy Spirit will touch those who read this testimony. For those who have been or may still be in any of these situations, I pray the Power of the Blood of Jesus will flow into the deep, hidden places and set you free! In Jesus Name, Amen.

Chapter I

Childhood Memories

I was born and raised in Birmingham, Alabama. My daddy was a brick mason, and my mother was a homemaker. Our home was always a happy home, filled with lots of love and activity. I have a few memories of the little two-bedroom house where I was born, but most all of my memories are from the home my daddy built back in 1959, where my parents still live today. I was 4 years old when we moved into the new home. I remember being so excited. The house was so big and beautiful. We had a huge back yard and woods to play in because our home was one of the first homes to be built there. We had gone from a little two-bedroom home to a four bedroom, two bath, big living room and dining room, plus a den and kitchen. We thought we were in a mansion!

Growing up in my house as a young child, I never felt like anything was missing. I never recall hearing my parents fuss or fight. My mom and dad always showed love to each other and to all of us children. They laughed, hugged, and teased each other a lot. Dad never left the house without kissing my mother goodbye. I grew up in a family of love.

My mom and dad had six children. I had two sisters and three brothers. I was number two with an older sister. My older sister and I shared a room because we were the two girls closest in age, just 18 months apart. I must admit; I probably wasn't the best roommate. My sister was neat and organized, and I was the total opposite. I was what you might call messy and out of the box! She would seriously draw a line down the middle of the dresser, the closet, the bed, and anywhere she could to separate my stuff from hers. It was great!

This left my youngest sister with a room all to herself. Since she could not share a room with one of my brothers, she got the private room. We all felt she was the lucky one. All three boys had to share a room, which is probably why my youngest brother was always found sleeping on the floor outside my mom and dad's bedroom door in the mornings.

We looked like an army everywhere we went, but boy, could we have fun! When we played games, we pretty much had a team already. We played outside a lot and met lots of friends. We always had some kind of pet, a dog, a rabbit, and even a flying squirrel.

Mother always dressed us so amazing. I don't know how she did it with six kids. She made a lot of our dresses. At Easter time, we all looked like a million dollars.

One thing that stands out in my mind is how we traveled. We did not have a big van or an SUV, just a regular car. Can you imagine eight people traveling from Alabama to Panama City, Florida in a car? Daddy would be driving, and mother was in the passenger seat with a child with no seat belt in the middle of them. There would be two kids lying in the back seat, two lying on the floor, and one at the back window. Amazing! I loved those trips. The beach has always been my favorite place to be. We would go there with all our relatives. We had so much fun. I have fond childhood memories with my family.

We went to church every Sunday morning. Our family sat on the right side of the church on the second row. We took up the whole pew. It became known as the Jones family pew. We went to church on Sunday evenings and during the week, especially on Wednesdays, which was choir day and dinner night.

I was raised in the Southern Baptist church. My daddy built the church and was a deacon there. I have so many memories connected to that church, including friends that I met in kindergarten. Memories of singing in the choir, going on retreats, vacation Bible school, and so much more. But most importantly, I came to the Lord and was baptized in that church on April 19, 1965, when I was 10 years old. I will never forget that day.

Another fond memory I have of Sundays is after church we would go to my grandparent's house for lunch, and all my cousins and aunts and uncles would be there. That was the best time ever. There is nothing better than home cooked southern food. I always liked to look in my grandmother's refrigerator because she always kept real chocolate milk that was delivered to her house by the milkman. She would have the best cheese wrapped in white paper from the little neighborhood store up the street. These were two of my favorite things, and it was always there.

We would have all of our big family holiday gatherings at our grandparent's house. Christmas was and is my favorite holiday. We would get there on Christmas Eve. My grandparents would have a real tree that they had cut down from somewhere out in the country. It would reach all the way to the ceiling. It was amazing! I remember a big record player in the corner of the room with Christmas music playing. My grandmother, mom, and all of my aunts would be cooking in the kitchen. There were kids running all over the place with excitement. I loved my grandparents. I loved being in their home. It was a warm, loving place to be.

Childhood Trauma

When we went to visit my other grandparents (my daddy's mom and dad), I remember going down a steep dirt road when we turned off to go to their house. When we got to the bottom, we could see the house. There was a really big field to the left side of the house. One time all of our relatives came over, and we played a game of baseball in that field. I remember my uncle broke his leg that day. There were lots of trees also, fruit trees as I recall. I remember picking blackberries from the fence alongside the road. That was one of my favorite things to do. I still love blackberries. There was also this great tire swing that my grandfather made out back for him to swing us on. It was so much fun because we could go so high. Sometimes my granddad would take us to the trees to pick the fruit. He would pick us up so we could reach it. I was always uncomfortable with the way he picked me up, but I couldn't explain why at the time.

I loved my grandmother. She was sweet and quiet. She cooked delicious little apple and peach pies that were shaped like omelets. She also made great cornbread. If you have never tried potluck, (turnip greens and cornbread) you don't know what you're missing! That was one of my daddy's favorite things to eat, and she would make it for him when we went over.

One day, our grandparents came to visit us at our house. This was a special occasion for me because they rarely came. My grandmother did not drive and never even got a driver's license. My daddy also had a brother who needed around the clock care. He was in a wheelchair due to an accident at birth. My grandmother took care of him, so we only saw my grandparents when we all went to see them.

My parents and my grandparents sat in our den and talked while we kids played. I cannot tell you who made the decision to go somewhere. Kids are always wanting to do something fun, and besides, we were with our grandfather, someone we trusted. He was a good Christian man. We lived about a mile or so from our community park and pool. We could ride our bikes, play ball, and swim. Everyone in our neighborhood knew each other, so we could walk there and back alone. It was safe. But for some reason that day, we must have walked down there with our granddaddy. I don't know of any other way we ended up there. My parents were not there, and I don't remember riding in a car. I just remember walking. I guess we wanted to show him the park. It was me, my older sister, and my brother that is a year younger than me. I don't remember any other kids being there.

As we were leaving to walk back home, we saw some unfinished homes on the street next to the park. Now, I can't recall if my grandfather suggested that we look inside one of the homes, or if it was us kids who wanted to go. I do know growing up around my daddy building houses, going inside of unfinished homes was a lot of fun. So, we all went inside. We were all just running around all through the place as kids do when I suddenly found myself alone with my granddad. He grabbed me, and I couldn't get away. My brother and sister were nowhere in sight. I remember standing in an opening where a window was going to be. I do not know why I remember that, except that I was looking for my sister and brother. Where were they? I needed help, but they never came.

He grabbed my hands as he opened his pants. Things began to happen. I was frozen with fear. My heart was pounding out of my chest. What was happening? I could not think or move. He was whispering in my ear that he loved me the whole time. The sound of his voice made me even more fearful. I did not say a word. To this day, I don't recall even leaving that unfinished house or the walk back home.

My Life Was Changed

From the day that happened to me, I felt fear and shame. I was so afraid because the person who had done this to me was my granddaddy. As a child, I had no idea what to do, so I kept silent. When you keep silent, you start building a wall around your heart. That's the only way you know how to protect yourself. I slowly began to feel myself change. I remember being sad when I was never sad before. The innocent, playful little girl I once was, was now gone. All I was left with was a memory that brought me fear. I did not know what to do with it. I just wanted it to go away, but it would not. Who would I go to with something like this? Who would truly listen and help me? What if it happened again? Who would believe that a family member that everybody loved had done this?

Even though we did not go to my grandparents very often, I remember seeing my grandfather after he violated me. I can't even put into words how I felt. I did not even have to see him. All it took was to hear his voice, and fear would set in.

The fear kept getting worse. In my heart, I was terrified of being near my own grandfather. It was very sad for a little girl to love someone and be afraid of them at the same time. I can vaguely remember times when I would hurt myself, like pulling my hair out or injuring the skin around my nails. I never understood why I was doing it, but it started after the incident with my grandfather. I was afraid of anyone getting too close to me. Fear grew deeper inside of me, and I noticed I feared things that never scared me before. I had no problem being around boys who were my childhood friends, but if I ever found out one liked me as a boyfriend, I never spoke to him again.

Not only was I afraid to be liked by boys, I was becoming increasingly afraid of other things too. Water was a big one. I can't explain why, and I don't know if it had anything to do with me being violated, but I was fearful of being underwater and not being able to breath. This fear kept me from learning to be a good swimmer. Our parents took us to have swimming lessons once, but it was hard for me to learn how to swim because I was so afraid of the water. Later in life, it robbed me of a lot of fun things. When I was married, we went to the lake a lot. I missed out on learning how to water ski. Fear just causes you to miss out on so much in life.

Bridges were another fear of mine. I had trouble walking across a bridge. Even driving over one, I would have panic attacks. I also had an issue with anyone grabbing my hands. If I was ever playing or wrestling around and someone would hold my hands down, it would set something off in me, and I would panic. When I would sit or sleep, I kept my hands clenched in a tight fist. I did this my entire life. I was also terrified of death and afraid to be closed in a coffin.

Fear had changed my life.

Our loved ones, moms, dads, grandparents, aunts, and uncles are the ones we should be able to trust. When there is a breach of trust in one of these relationships, major wounds are created in the entire family. I trusted my granddaddy. Before that incident, I never had any reason not to, but now that trust had been broken and could never be restored. I had an open wound in my heart, and I was scared and afraid to trust. It turned me into a sad and afraid little girl. I went to bed every night and got up every day keeping my little secret, pretending things were okay.

Uncovering the Secret

One day, my mom and dad wanted to talk to my brothers and sisters and me. They were calling us into their bedroom one by one, shutting the door behind them. We had no idea what was going on because we had never seen our parents do anything like this before. We all knew something serious was going on. When it was my turn to go in, I remember my mom and dad sitting on the edge of their bed. In a nice calm voice, they asked me if my granddaddy had ever touched me in any way that was inappropriate. I was not expecting that at all. I started to cry and couldn't stop. By my reaction, they knew something had happened. So, I told them what I could remember about the day my grandfather violated me. I was sad to have to tell my daddy that.

After the secret about what had happened to me got out, we stopped going to visit my grandparents. Mother and daddy felt the need to keep a closer eye on all of us kids. I am not sure of my exact age when the incident with my grandfather occurred, but I am pretty sure I was no more than eight years old. That means my oldest sister would have been around 9 or 10, so she was able to recall things about that time better than I was. She said that my grandparents came to visit us a few times after the secret was exposed, but I don't remember. All I knew was there seemed to be no consequences or healing for this horrible thing that had happened to me. So, now I was thinking, "Was what happened to me okay?" I was tormented in my mind, and it seemed that everyone I knew and loved had returned to life as usual.

And then, everyone got silent. No one talked about it anymore. Life just went back to "normal." I guess that's just the way things were done back then. If you did not talk about what happened, then you must be ok, and it just goes away. I don't remember anything being said or done to help me heal. No one asked me about what happened ever again. No one asked me how I was doing or if I was okay. Did anyone even notice the change in me? It seemed like things had just been swept under the rug.

As a little girl, I will tell you, I never stopped hearing the sound of my granddaddy's voice— it haunted me at times. I don't think my parents really understood the effect that one traumatic moment had on my life. So, I learned how to lock those fears deep down inside of me. I tried my best not think about it ever again, even though I lost a piece of my heart that day, leaving me with a big hole in its place. But I just kept moving forward, not knowing the destruction that hole would bring later down the road.

Chapter 2

Love & Marriage

Besides that one incident with my grandfather, I had a very protected and sheltered upbringing. I never really ventured far outside of my neighborhood. I hung out with friends that I had known since kindergarten. There were probably about eight of us girls that were best friends, and we hung out together for years.

I loved the outdoors, and I loved to run. I could outrun any boy barefooted. I didn't care for shoes in the summer. I loved climbing trees and riding skateboards, and we didn't have flat streets in Alabama. We had lots of big hills. I loved playing softball, and I would have played more sports if more had been offered to young girls in the 70's.

I loved sleep overs with my girlfriends. We would stay up late at night and talk about fun things like cute boys. I loved looking at teen magazines. I thought it was so neat to see the different hair styles and cloths. I loved fashion. Those were new and exciting times!

By now, our home was full of teenagers. My younger sister was 13, my brother was 14, I was 15, and my oldest sister was 17. Talking about a crazy time in the Jones' house! My sister was already in high school by then, and I was ready for my freshman year. I felt like our house was full of crazy hormones going all over the place.

My sister was the first sibling to get a car, probably to help mother out, even though I don't remember riding to school with her very much because we went at different times. I rode with a girlfriend from down the street name Charbett. She would come by and pick me up.

Another funny thing I remember, especially with so many teenagers in the house, is we only had one phone. It hung on the wall in our kitchen. Our kitchen was open to our den area, where everybody always was, so there was never ever any privacy. We would stretch that phone cord as far as we could outside to our patio. That was the longest phone cord we had ever seen! That phone is still hanging on the wall there and still being used today.

One of the things that got me through many days and nights was music. I absolutely love music. It is one of my greatest passions. In my early teens, I was deeply touched by soul music. I can't explain it, but it reached places way down deep inside of me. I would relate to the words in the songs and to the rhythm it carried. It moved me. It would just make me feel good and loved. I fell in love with Motown records. I loved all the artists and the music. I loved to watch all the dance shows on TV and learn the dance moves. When we had dances at our school, it was fun to know all the new dances. I used to dance all through the house. My dad would say, "Girl you dance everywhere you go!" Music just brought out the best in me, fun, love, and sometimes even tears.

Sorority Days

It was an exciting time! It was the summer before starting high school. I was 15 years old, and I would be leaving my small group of friends. And even though they were all going with me, we would now be spread out among about 1000 other students. Wow! How scary and exciting it was to go from being the big eighth grader to the little freshman. Everybody could always recognize a freshman. We always stood out. We either looked afraid, didn't dress right, or we were always lost, but everyone knew who we were.

One of the most exciting things about high school for me was the sororities you could rush for. Some really popular girls from my church were members of one of them, and they had told me how great it was to be a part of it. Plus, to be a part of a sorority, you were involved in community events, school events, big fund raisers, and trips to Florida Sorority week. Being in this sorority meant you were connected. I really loved the thought of being a part of something like this. One day at church, one of the girls I knew came up to me and told me the sorority was voting, and my name had made the cut. I was so excited, but I also knew that they only voted in about 4 to 6 girls out of all the girls coming into the high school at the beginning of the year. Then they would rush again at the end of the year. So now, I just had to wait and see.

Then one Saturday morning, I was fast asleep in my bed when I was awakened by a bunch of screaming girls telling me to get up and come with them. I had to go just as I was, in pajamas and rollers (yes, we wore rollers back then). I could not brush my teeth or my hair. The sorority was gathering up all the girls they had voted in to rush. They took us to one of the girl's home, told us who our big sisters would be, and gave us instructions on what our rush week would look like, which did not sound so good. Some of the older sorority girls really took advantage of us that week, but overall most of them were very good to us.

I opened myself up to this because I needed a something safe to be connected to. I needed a group of people that I would feel safe with, and since I already knew some of the girls, it was familiar to me. One girl named Janey had been my best friend all my life. It made the big high school not seem so big to me.

Dating Years

Being in a sorority was also an extra bonus when it came to getting dates. All the older girls knew all the best-looking guys, and they were always trying to get them dates.

I will never forget the first date I ever went on. Who could ever forget their first date. We went to a

Sweetheart Banquet on or around Valentine's Day. Oh my goodness, when I think about that day! Everything was horrible. I remember having this fancy up-do (yes up-do). I wore a long formal blue lace dress, and I believe I had on those long white gloves. Oh my goodness, My date brought me flowers and even a huge box of chocolates! My mom was in love. We had a double date, and they wanted to go out to eat after the banquet. He ordered me shrimp cocktail. At that time in my life, I don't think I had ever eaten that before. So, that did not go well. I can't even remember talking to him much at all. I was so afraid I would say the wrong thing. I talked to Jan, the other girl that was with us, and thank goodness she was! When he brought me home, I just said, "Thank you," and went inside.

I was never very concerned about dating in high school, even though it seemed like the opportunity was always there. To me, it was just as much fun to go out with a group of friends to the football games or to McDonalds where we used to all hang out. We had lots of sorority parties, and sometimes it was more fun if you did not have a date. My dating years in high school were fun, innocent years, which consisted mainly of going to football games, homecomings, basketball games, baseball games, or maybe even a date to a church function. My freshman to junior years were still years of innocence for me. Those were fun, good times.

Falling in Love

It was now the summer of 1972, just after my junior year of high school. School had been going great. I had met so many friends, even some from surrounding schools that our school competed against. I still liked my sorority, but I had been making new friends in other areas of my life outside the sorority. My taste for music was growing. I was loving the new music. I was all over the place, from The Temptations, Bee Gees, Marvin Gaye, and Roberta Flack, to Led Zeppelin, Creedence Clearwater Revival, The Doobie Brothers, and the Lynyrd Skynyrd band. I loved music. My sister always had cool music. She liked all the hippie stuff, black lights, and posters, so she had all that stuff in our room. Our room was half that and half my preppy sorority stuff. How funny!

I had made a new friend, but she was not a part of the sorority. Linda was a cheerleader at our school. We found we had a lot in common and became best friends. There was nothing we could not talk about. She was so different from any other girlfriend I had ever had. She was never jealous of me, and I was never jealous of her. We always brought out the best in each other, were always there for each other, and always looking out for each other. She is still there for me if I call today. A good friend will never leave you when times are bad. She is my friend forever. I love her very much.

In June of that same year, I got a phone call from my friend Lauren. She was an older friend that I had met from another school. She said she needed me to do her a really big favor. She wanted me to go on a blind date with a college guy from the University of Alabama. She said that he was a super nice guy, and he was an Alabama cheerleader. She said I would be on a double date, and the other guy was also an Alabama cheerleader. She assured me I would not be alone and that I would be safe because she knew that I did not do blind dates. Besides, she said I might know the other guy I would be on the double date with. His name was Don Waits. He had graduated from Banks High School. She had fixed him up with a friend of hers. I told her that I already had plans for that day. I had a lunch date that I could not cancel. But Lauren was a very persuasive person. She begged me to go. She said she would owe me big time. I did not know Don, but I had heard of him, so I agreed.

Later that day, I got a call from a guy named Jimmy asking me out on this blind date. He seemed like a really nice guy. He said we were going bowling and asked me if that was ok. That sounded good to me. I wasn't a stranger to the bowling alleys. As kids, we would go with my dad when he would play on his bowling leagues. He would get us our own lane to play on. So, I loved to bowl.

I went on my lunch date that afternoon. Then later that evening, I got ready for my blind date. I was not worried at all because I had never gone on a blind date because I never liked the idea of it. So, I wasn't really expecting very much from it. I was basically doing a good friend a favor.

In the 70's, everything we wore was really short. I had on this little mini dress with matching bottoms. I remembered it was so cute, but not for bowling! It was in style, so it must have been ok, or I am sure my mom and dad would not have let me out the door. So, Jimmy came and picked me up. His friend Don was driving a convertible. I remember getting in and sitting in the front seat on the console next to Don with no seat belt. We were all in the front driving over to pick up Don's date. I remember talking to Don a lot in the car. Maybe talking to the one who was not your date was easier. When we got to the bowling alley, we were all having a lot of fun, and Jimmy, my date, was a really nice guy. But Don and I kept talking and looking at each other. There was an attraction between the two of us, and I knew Jimmy could tell.

The next morning was June 23, 1972. I believe we were celebrating my sister's birthday. I remember my grandmother being there. We were all in the living room when our private phone in our bedroom rang. My grandmother had gotten my sister and I our own private phone line and number. My sister went to answer it. She came back and said, "The phone is for you, and its Don Waits. What does he want?"

All excited, I ran back to my room and grabbed the phone and said, "yes" to our first date. He had asked his friend Jimmy if he could ask me out. Jimmy said yes, and Don called me the very next day.

To be honest, I don't really remember what we did on our first date. I think we went to a movie, and if it's the movie I am thinking of in my mind, it was not the best movie to take a seventeen-year-old young lady to in downtown Alabama. I remember being a little nervous, but I went where he went. Everything about him was new to me. He thought different, his ways were different, and he seemed to be outside of my little world, even though we only lived about a mile from each other. I had feelings that I had never experienced before. I had dated many guys, but never someone that I could not get off my mind. I thought of him all day long. I waited for his call just to hear his voice. I wanted to see him and be with him all the time.

It was the summer before his sophomore year of college and the summer before I would be a senior in high school. It was the summer that life took a complete turn for me. My life changed, and my eyes were opened and introduced to new things. One of those things was drinking while at Don's home one evening while his parents were gone. I could have made the choice not to drink, but I didn't.

Crazy in Love

I was so crazy in love over the summer that I had not accepted any other dates from any other boys. I just wasn't interested in anyone else. Don was working a summer job during the day, and we were together every chance we got. We would talk on the phone for hours. Sometimes I would just go to bed with the phone to my ear or the pillow over my head so my parents would not know how long we talked. I would wake up with the phone still there.

We did the craziest things. There were times when I would climb out my window (the old fashion roll out windows) at night to meet with him when my parents were asleep. I would find any way to be with him. His parents had a lake house, and we would go up there for the day for a date to be together. That was a lot of fun! I can remember hearing Elton John's Tiny Dancer playing in the car. We went on picnics and did a lot of things with our families.

When school started again, everything changed. I didn't get to see Don during the week anymore. I only saw him on weekends when he would come home from college. Sometimes his parents didn't even know he was coming home. I couldn't stand not seeing him all the time. It was hard to talk on the phone because it was now a long-distance phone call. Things were getting hard. I couldn't wait until I could see him on the weekends. I just wanted to be with him all the time. For the first time in my life, I had fallen madly in love.

One day, Don asked me if I would be able to come to the college with him some weekends. They always had concerts or parties and things to do there. This was going to take a lot of persuading my parents, especially my mom. She was pretty careful about where she let us kids go. Dad was a little more lenient. I was still 17 at the time, just a few months shy of 18, but I had never done anything for them to not trust me.

There was some big fraternity party coming up, and Don wanted me to come with him. He told my parents everything was set up for me to stay with sorority girls. My parents were familiar with high school sororities, but this was college. But they felt it was safe and agreed to let me go. I had never been so excited! It was my first time ever going to a big college. My first time ever to be away from home like that. The first time I had ever traveled to another town with my boyfriend, staying with people in an unfamiliar place. It was such a big deal to me. You would have thought I was leaving the country.

But when we got there, things had changed. Turns out, I didn't have a place to stay other than with him. He explained that the plans had fallen through. Fear suddenly set in. I can't explain why. I wasn't sure if the plans had really fallen through or if the plans to stay with him were the plans all along. I felt deceived and stuck in the situation. It wasn't like I could just leave and go back home. The issue I had with trust resurfaced, but I quickly tried to put it away because I was so in love with him. I refused to believe anything was going on or anything bad was going to happen to me.

I remember the sleeping situation affected the way I acted at the party. Most of the time, I sat around watching other people having a good time. I was the quiet one observing what was going on, keeping a wall around myself to keep me protected. I was exposed to a lot of things that weekend, and I was just trying to absorb it all. It was a way of living that I was not brought up in and had never been exposed to. It was a critical time in my life where I was trying to make some serious decisions. I was madly in love with this 20-year-old college boy who was living a completely different lifestyle than I was. I was battling some incredible emotions inside, but the love I had for him was so strong, it would not let go.

We went back to his place or the place we were staying at the time and went to sleep. Nothing happened. I felt so much better the next day. He showed me around the campus, and we had a fun weekend.

When I got home, of course the first thing my mom asked was, "How was your trip?" Having to make up a story about girls I stayed with that didn't exist had to be one of the worst things I had ever done. My mom and I were very close. Lying to her made me feel horrible. I had never lied and made up a story like that before. Even though nothing happened, there was no way I could have told her we stayed together. It would have crushed her heart, and my dad would not have liked it at all. Keeping secrets is a horrible thing!

I had such mixed emotions. On one hand, I knew I really loved him and nothing bad had happened, but then on the other hand, I had not told the truth, and I felt totally uncomfortable. There was such a battle going on inside of me.

Demands

My parents were so excited that the first trip went so well, they trusted me to go more often. We sort of rotated weekends. One weekend I met one of his roommates and thought he would be an awesome date for my best friend, so we introduced them. They fell in love and are still married today.

I got involved in the college scene. I started trying whatever Don was doing and that included drugs. We would go to rock concerts where it was normal to see drinking, smoking, and drugs. I can't even begin to list the number of times I found myself in dangerous situations. One night, we were in the car coming back from a concert, and everyone was passed out. I woke up to find the driver driving on the center median of the highway. I knew I wasn't making the best the decisions, but I did not care. I just wanted to be with Don. It was hard keeping things from your parents, but for me, it was worth it to be with him.

Don and I had been together now for about 9 months, I had turned 18 that January, and he was now 21. He was getting frustrated with our relationship because we had not been intimate. I will never forget the day he told me that he would have to stop seeing me if we could not be together in that way. I had never been so afraid of losing someone in my entire life. So, now I had this huge decision to make. Would I go against everything I was taught? That is not what my mother had done, and that was not what she had taught me. But I was scared to death of him walking away.

He always told me he loved me. I believed him when he said it. He said he loved me so much that he couldn't continue to be with me without truly being with me. I desperately loved him and wanted to be with him always. So, I chose to go against what I knew was right and gave in to his demands so I would not lose him, believing we would become even closer.

Shattered Heart

I won't go into detail about that night, but I will say this, it was no honeymoon after your beautiful wedding day with all your friends and family. Nothing about it was romantic. It was being totally afraid, but doing it anyway because I truly loved him with all my heart, and I trusted that he loved me because he said he did. Everything was just emotional. It's hard to explain. When I got home that weekend, I felt like my parents were going to know exactly what had happened. For some reason, I felt because something on the inside of me had changed that everyone was going to think that I looked different on the outside too. I wasn't at all comfortable with what I had done.

Even the girls in my high school sorority were making comments about me dating a college guy. I think they were noticing the changes in me. I was losing interest in all the high school activities and the sorority functions. They even came and talked to my mom one day. I finally got tired of it all and lost total interest in anyone that got involved in my business.

My girlfriend had also gotten really serious with Don's roommate, so we were hanging out all the time. This made it even more fun. Since Linda and I were best friends, I had someone to talk to, and she could talk to me. We could talk to each other about everything and anything that had to do with those two boys. When we weren't with them, we had each other to hang out with. During the week, we would make new outfits to wear on the weekends. It was perfect! Linda could sew faster than I could, so I would cut out the patterns, and she would sew. We would make halter tops and dresses. We made a great team.

One weekend, we were all planning to get together when Don called me and said he would not be able to come and get me. He had way too much studying to do for his finals. I was really sad because I always looked forward to seeing him. I called Linda and she was still going, so my plans were the only ones that had suddenly changed. I never heard from any of them over the weekend, but when they got back, my friend Linda had something to tell me.

She told me that Don had not been studying for finals. He had company that weekend. What she saw put an image in my mind that never went away. He was caught in the act with a dark-haired girl in the bathtub. I was so shocked and devastated that I didn't know how to respond or what to do. I was mad, and I hated him for lying to me. All I could think about was me giving myself to Don, and all I felt was shame. I felt what we had was all a lie and what I had done with him was for no reason. At that moment, I truly wanted to die. That was something I never thought I would ever hear of him doing. It never ever entered my mind. I was tricked, betrayed, and lied to. I was sad and hurt, and I didn't know what to do.

That next weekend there was a party in town with some pre-med friends that Don and his roommate knew. Once again, Don did not come home, but his roommate did, and both Linda and I went to the party. I was still an emotional mess. It was probably not the best place for me to be, but I wanted to get out and to not think about what had happened. I was still angry and hurt with him, and he was still not coming home to face what he had done. Because these guys that were having the party had access to pharmaceutical drugs, they gave me a bag of them to give to Don. They trusted me as his girlfriend to give them to him. Well, during the party, I decided to take some. I remember taking two and having a drink of vodka. A little while later, I took two more while still drinking. I remember getting two more out of the bag and taking them and some guy handing me another drink. That was the last thing I remembered.

The drug that I was taking was called Quaalude (Methaqualone). Back then, in the '70's, we called them Ludes or Sopers. One tablet was 300 mg. A dose of 8,000 is lethal, however 2,000 could be lethal, especially mixed with alcohol.

I had no recollection of how many I had taken or how much I had had to drink. No one was watching me. We were all partying, and no one knew what I was doing until it was too late. I was so hurt that I only thought of how I was feeling. I wanted the picture of the pain in my head to go away. I never intended to hurt anyone else. That night, as I lay there lifeless from drugs and alcohol, I gave my best friend, her boyfriend, and all his buddies at the party quite a scare. They were all trying to revive me. It was not what anyone had planned on doing that night. To this day, my girlfriend can't even recall all the details. It's probably for the best. It was not a good night. They called Don to let him know what was going on and from what she remembered, he was angry. He thought someone else had done it to me.

Later, I remember thinking back on how grateful I was that the pre-med guys were there. I don't know what all they did that night, but they knew how to help me. I am so thankful my girlfriend was there with me too.

Rebellion

When I saw Don again, we got into a big argument over this incident. He was so mad about what I had done. He was mad at me for the drug incident, and I was mad about what he had done with the other girl to cause it. We were going in circles. I don't think he understood how traumatic the situation with him and the dark-haired girl was for me and how it truly affected me. A deep, disturbing, damaging, devastating heartbreak took place. It was actually the very beginning of a lifetime of distrust.

And never once did I get an apology from the person that I loved so much. Not once was he sorry that he hurt me. Not once did he ask me to forgive him for breaking my heart. That's all I wanted and needed at the time, but I got nothing. I had nothing to help me with the pain I felt.

The overdose was a terrible thing that happened. A terrible situation that I had gone through, and now I was feeling guilty and bad about it. Instead of talking about why it happened, I felt ashamed of what I had done. My mom and dad did not even know any of this had occurred. Not even my sisters or brothers knew. No one other than my girlfriend and those who were there to help knew what happened that night. It was another secret that just got swept under the rug. There was no one to talk to for help. I had my girlfriend, and that was all.

I guess you could say Don and I worked things out, or at least we moved forward, and I was thankful for that. I never ever wanted to lose my relationship with him. I wish there had been someone who could have helped us both get some much-needed healing. I have to say that things changed after that incident, at least it did for me. The feeling of being totally special to him was all messed up now. I just did not feel like I was truly that one special, beautiful girl he would say I was. Now that he had cheated, it didn't make sense to me. I didn't know what I meant to him anymore. It didn't matter how beautiful or special he said I was, it wasn't the same now that I knew he could say that one day and be with someone else the next. I was lost and confused as to why I was the one he loved, yet I wasn't good enough. But I still wanted to be with him because I knew he loved me. I had no doubt about that, but he did not love me enough to be satisfied with just me. I started to compare myself with the other girls I would see at the college.

Once, one of his roommates (not the one dating my girlfriend) told me how Don really liked dark haired girls. Well, I am blonde. I was even more upset when I heard that. I was just having a really hard teenage time with my own self confidence. It didn't matter to me if others thought I was the most beautiful person ever, it was what I thought and felt about myself that was developing my personality.

I was still so in love with Don, but sometimes, when you get so hurt in love you do really dumb stuff. There was a place in my heart that became a little numb. I guess I just put up another area of that wall so I could protect myself again. Here was another man, this time a young man that I was crazy in love with, taking pieces of my heart, and I didn't know of anything else to do but build a wall to help me stay safe.

I started giving myself more freedom when I was at home. This is something I had not done before. Usually, everything I did was with the girls or about Don. But now, I decided it was ok to party, and if it was ok for him to do as he pleased, then it was ok for me. I started drinking with friends at parties, which I normally did not do unless I was away with him. I basically did as I pleased. I wasn't very good at it, but I was just trying to prove that I was not going to sit around and be anyone's dummy. I did not really care about anyone else, nor did I really want to go out with anyone else. But this time, if he didn't call or come home, I was not going to look like the fool.

We continued to date through my final months of high school. I had such a strong attraction to him that no matter what had gone on, I still wanted to be with him. Our problem was never solved, however. We never healed. We just put a big bandage on top of it and moved on. Another issue swept under the rug. At that time, the use of drugs was really wide spread. I could take the downers and not care about anything that was going on, and that was what I was doing. I could not fix the problem or get it out of my head, but I could take something that made me not care about it, and I could love this person and not be mad. I could have fun and be happy.

The drugs helped me cope when I had no help, but they were only masking the issue. They were a fad, not something I could continue to do all my life. I just loved being with Don. I didn't care what we were doing, I just wanted to be together. Towards the end of May, it was time for me to graduate from high school. Don would still be going to school during the summer to finish up his college year. We had a decision to make and this time, I really rebelled against my parents.

Living Together

We were so in love with each other. There was no way we wanted to go another summer just seeing each other on weekends. I had graduated, so I had no school now. I was free for the summer. Don decided that I should move in with him that summer while he finished school. Oh my gosh, I could not imagine doing that, but the thought of being together every day was so exciting. At the same time, I knew my mother would have an absolute fit, and I was sure my dad wouldn't like it either. But there I was again, it was all about me and what I needed for myself, and I needed to be with him. So, I of course I said, "Yes!"

My dad was not happy about it, but he knew there was no stopping me. He knew how much I loved Don. My mom was so unhappy about what I was doing that she stopped speaking to me all together. After I packed my things and left, she never spoke to me again the whole time I was gone, even when I would call home to check on them. My dad would talk to me and tell me how everyone was doing, but not mom. I really hurt her. She was very disappointed in my decision to live with someone outside of marriage. I was turning against every spiritual thing I had ever been taught by my parents. I walked away from their authority and protection because I felt all grown up.

We were there together for about four months while he finished school. We got along great. I guess it was like a newlywed couple in their first home, except we weren't married. I loved being with him all the time. There was no doubt in my mind that I wanted to be with him for the rest of my life. You know this in your heart when you just can't imagine your life without someone, and he was that someone to me.

Even though we were having an amazing time together, deep inside I had mixed feelings. I always felt strange, especially around family. I knew our living situation was grieving our parents back home. That was not a good feeling for me. I never wanted to hurt my parents, and I certainly didn't want his parents to think badly of me, so that was always there in the back of my mind.

On the college campus, it felt ok to live that way because everyone else was doing it. It was like we were in our own little happy world there. It's so amazing how love will make you do the craziest things in life, even when it goes against everything you were raised to believe.

One weekend, his parents called and invited us to meet them at the lake house, and we decided to go. I had always loved going there. Little did I know, they had planned to have some serious conversations with us about the lifestyle we were living. His dad took him out on the boat and had a talk with him about his intentions and what his plans were. They just simply told us that we were good people that had been raised better than the way we were living. Good people didn't do the things we were doing and live the way we were living. Of course, they were not telling me anything that I did not already know. It wasn't like we had never talked about getting married someday. It's just that we had never made any serious plans about it, like setting a date. Besides, he was not finished with school yet.

After that trip to the lake house, he came into the room one day with three little pieces of paper folded up inside a baseball cap. He said, "Pick one!" So, I did. I opened it up and saw November 16 written on it. He said, "That's the day we are getting married!" Yes, that's the unique way our wedding day was picked, November 16,1974.

He finished up school, graduated from college, and we packed our things and headed home, but this is where it got rough. He went to his home, and I went to mine. We only lived about a mile or so from each other, but being together every day and then apart was truly difficult.

Wedding Plans

My parents were happy that I was back home, and most of all, happy that there was now going to be a wedding. This was a good time for my mom and I to get some much-needed healing time. I had really missed my mom. I talked to her pretty much every day, and I had truly missed that.

So now all the fun of planning the wedding had begun. I had a church wedding in the church I grew up in, and it was also the church that my daddy built. The pastor that married us was the same pastor that married my mom and dad. I was so excited that he was able to be there to join us together before the Lord. We had a typical Southern wedding, about 250 guests and about 20 in the wedding party. It was very beautiful. Everything that led up to the wedding, the parties, lunches, gatherings with both the families and friends was so exciting. It was more than a girl could have ever dreamed, wished for, or expected to have.

My dress was perfect! My flowers were perfect! I had roses and they trailed all the way down about a foot. My wedding cake was absolutely gorgeous, and the groom's cake was amazing. Just layers and layers of chocolate with fruit cascading down the sides. I love roses, so all the girls in the wedding carried a rose. Everything about that day was perfect. I was marrying the love of my life. It was the best day of my life.

There was nothing like being married. I was so happy and so proud to be called Mrs. Waits. I loved fixing up our little apartment. His parents had given us their old bedroom furniture. I thought it was the most beautiful furniture ever. I was so excited to have it. We went to this place that sold unpainted furniture and found a table and chairs that we both loved. We bought it and worked on staining it together. It turned out beautiful. I loved it and was so proud of it.

His dad gave us a couch that fell off of a truck. It had no legs, so we put brick blocks underneath it to lift it up. We thought it looked great. We had Alabama Power spools for our end tables, and I made pretty material coverings to hang over them. There was nothing I wouldn't do to make our home look amazing. I will never forget our first Christmas there. Our tree was so heavy with decorations that it started to fall over, so Don tied it to the top of the curtain rod to hold it up. Those were such great times.

We were both working. Don's dad had helped me get an interview with an insurance company where he knew some people. I had very little work experience and only my high school diploma, so I had very few options in the work force. I applied for the filling department and was hired. My boss was an elderly lady who didn't seem to care much about us younger girls. I can just remember it was a very strict place to work, and you were not even allowed to go to the restroom without asking her permission.

We had one car, so Don dropped me off at work. He would go to work and come back to pick me up. It was fun to talk about all the things that happened during our day. I loved making plans for our future. I loved being married.

Chapter 3

Traumatic Loss

After being married a few months, I got really sick. I had no idea what was going on. I just knew I wasn't feeling good at all. I started losing weight, and then I got even sicker and broke out into hives. I was red and swollen all over. I went to the doctor, and he treated the hives with medication, but I didn't get any better.

Someone asked if I might possibly be pregnant, but I was on the birth control pill at the time. I remembered a few months earlier, I had missed two doses, but I continued with the next dose as they said you could. So, I really never thought that could be what was wrong with me. But as I continued to feel worse, I thought, "Why not take a pregnancy test to be sure." So, I took it, and it was negative.

Weeks went by, and I was still not any better. My body was just not right. Something was definitely going on. We bought a second pregnancy test, and it still came out negative. So, I let it go, thinking for sure that was obviously not my problem.

I continued to feel worse, so I decided I needed to go see a doctor. I must admit, going to a doctor was not my favorite thing to do. I had a terrible fear of needles, and I hated the unknown of what the doctor would have to do or tell me.

I will never forget that doctor's appointment as long as I live. Even though I cannot recall all the details of that day, I can recall the devastating news I got. After examining me, the doctor told me that I was in fact pregnant, but he felt there was a problem that had caused me to be so sick. He explained the situation and told us that the fetus would likely not be normal. Finding out you are pregnant is supposed to be one of the happiest days of your life. For me, it was the most heartbreaking.

Abortion

I was completely devastated. I had so many questions in my mind that just wasn't ever going to be answered. Why didn't any of those pregnancy tests show that I was pregnant. I could have stopped taking the pill long before. Why did I get so sick with those hives? The doctor said the medication that they had given me to treat the hives was a mega dose and would have never been prescribed to someone that was pregnant. There were so many "whys" in my mind. I didn't want to have to make the choice they were asking me to make. Why couldn't everything just be ok and normal like it was supposed to be when a couple finds out they are having their first child?

We didn't talk to hardly anyone about it, but we did talk to our parents. They were very sad, but from what I can remember, they had no real advice to help us decide what we should do. I remember talking to Don's brother because he was in medical school at the time. We thought he could help us with what was going on if he knew the facts. We knew they would support us no matter what, but I was looking for an answer that I never got from anyone. We did the best we could with the horrible news that we had.

We were running out of time. I wasn't getting any better, and I was already so far along in the pregnancy that I was going to have to be in the hospital for the procedure. I just couldn't bring myself to decide. I couldn't handle what was happening to me, so Don had to be the strong one. With sadness in our hearts and no words to explain what we were going through, we followed the advice of the doctors and made the decision to terminate the pregnancy.

The appointment was made, and I arrived at the hospital. My mother was there with me. I am so thankful for her. She was always by my side, especially when I needed her most. I so did not want to be where I was. This should not be happening to me. I had only been married about 4 months. These were supposed to be happy times. This was not supposed to be happening!

The doctors came in and hooked me up to all these medications. Not long after that, I went into labor. To go into labor and know I would never see or hold my baby was so devastating and heartbreaking. I could have never imagined such pain. I felt like I might lose my mind just thinking about it. It was the most horrible thing I have ever had to go through in my life. It was a feeling you just wouldn't be able to understand unless it happened to you. I wanted to see my child, but they would not allow it. I wanted to know if it was a boy or a girl, but they would not tell me. It was my baby, and it was taken away without me being able to see what had been wrong with it. I needed to know that. Maybe they thought differently back then, but it would have helped me deal with the pain.

I was left with a gaping hole in my heart from losing my baby, and it could never be replaced. Oh God, how was that hole ever going to be healed? There was an empty place there now, and I didn't know how to fill it.

Migraines

After that, we went about life as usual. I was the type of person who kept my thoughts and feelings hidden inside. My heart was sad, and I didn't know how to fix it. I couldn't get back what was lost. It was hard for me to let go of things because I just sort of let them build up inside of me. I didn't have anyone to talk to or anywhere to go for help. We didn't talk about what happened at all anymore; it was like it never even happened. Our family did not ever mention it either. It was another thing swept under the rug. I wanted to talk about what had happened. I needed to talk about it. I was going crazy inside because I was always thinking about it. But instead, I had to go about my life like nothing had ever happened. Oh, dear God, how many more things would I be able to pile under this rug?

Losing my baby just became another open wound, just like all the other ones. Another wound that I had to put a bandage on to cover it up because there was no one or no place to go for help. It was a lot to deal with at just 19 years old.

I was a young teenage girl who had just gotten married and was so in love. I had already survived being molested, a drug overdose, and now letting go of my child. Outside of my world, no one knew anything about all of this. They only knew of the young girl who had just married the love of her life. To them, she was the happiest girl in the world, and everything looked so perfect. On the outside, everything always looked perfect. We were a beautiful couple, and there was never a question about my love for him.

Because I could not let go of the pain and the trauma of everything that had happened to me, I started to get sick. It seemed like everything affected my head. It's like the memory of things that bothered me would play over and over in my mind like a movie that wouldn't stop playing, and I would get frequent headaches. I remember one evening we had gone to a dinner banquet where my husband worked. I recall sitting there trying to engage with everyone and have a good time, but I had a horrible headache. As the evening went on, the headache continued to get worse. I had never had anything like this before in my life. Before I knew it, the pain became so severe that I could not even see, and then I passed out. I was taken to the hospital to find out that I was having a migraine. I had never experienced such horrible pain. I thought I was going to die, and it seemed like nothing they gave me made the pain go away.

That was the beginning of a nightmare for me. For 38 years, I suffered with debilitating migraine headaches. I probably saw more than 20 of the top neurologists. I had anywhere from 3 to 6 migraines a month, lasting 4 to 6 days each. I was on so many medications trying to manage the pain, I don't know how I functioned. I suffered 3 small strokes and memory loss. I was fearful to go anywhere, not knowing when I would get another migraine. I was told there was no cure, and I would be this way for the rest of my life.

Affair

It didn't take long. In fact, it was only two years into the marriage. I was still very much in love with my husband. That was never an issue. But there was a hurt burning deep inside of me, a hurt that had never been healed. Don's attitude and feelings about what had happened with the dark-haired girl before we were married just made things worse for me. It was an "it's just what guys do" attitude. I felt like I was now just one of all those girls, one of those "no big deals." I had a real problem with my heart being angry and hurt. I was very angry for never receiving an apology and for not seeing a change in his attitude. So, instead of me being loving and kind, I did just the opposite. I became just like him. I hardened my heart, and I made a choice to get even and pay him back. I decided if he could hurt me like that and not really think it mattered, I could do the same to him. I guess I thought it would shake him to his core. So, even though I had no clue how to even go about doing anything of this nature, I engaged in an affair with a co-worker.

It was strange and awkward, and instead of it accomplishing what I guess I thought it would, it totally backfired. All it caused was fighting, emotional abuse, and Don then felt he had permission to do the same to me.

Chapter 4

Starting Our Family

After being married a little over 5 years, we decided it was time to have children. I had never been so excited. It didn't take us long to conceive. The day I got the news, I was shouting from the mountain tops. We were both on cloud nine. Our parents were so happy. My husband made sure I was eating enough for two, but all that did was make me bigger. I gained 64 lbs. during that pregnancy. My doctor wasn't very happy with the concept of me eating for two. He explained that the baby would get what it needed, but we were just so excited we wanted to do everything right. I loved picking out baby names, fixing up the baby room, and looking at baby clothes. I was in Heaven, and my heart was happy.

The morning I went into labor, my husband wasn't home. He was a pilot, so he traveled a lot. So, I called my parents, and they came and took me to the hospital. They called the airport to let my husband know. My labor started early, around 5 am and went all day. The baby was not moving down the birth canal, and they couldn't figure out why. They got me up to walk in hopes that it would move the baby along. They even tried pushing him down with one nurse holding my legs and two nurses pushing the baby down. That was terribly painful, but nothing seemed to be working. There were times when the baby seemed to be under stress. The labor was just going way too long. My mom was there with me. Again, I was thankful that she was there. After 12 hours in labor, the doctor was getting concerned.

My mother, a mother of 6 children, was getting to see a birth for the first time in her life. It was so amazing! And then I heard the doctor say, "You have a son!" I had never seen anything as beautiful and amazing as that baby boy. He was absolutely perfect! Don rushed back from his trip and got there the minute he was born.

As he was being delivered, the doctor noticed the umbilical cord with a complete perfect knot wrapped around his neck. He said he had never seen one like that in his 23 years of practice. This was probably why the baby didn't drop. We had never done an ultrasound during the pregnancy because there was no reason to. Knots in the umbilical cord can tighten when the baby starts descending the birth canal, causing a true knot. This results in a definite increase in the risk of death of the baby and almost always results in a caesarean. Michael Chadwick was a miracle.

Michael Chadwick Waits was beautiful and perfect in every way. He was a gift from God. I had never been so happy. I wanted to hold him all the time. He was the best baby in the world. I stopped working outside the home when I was 8 months pregnant, and once he was born, I never went back. I never left him ever. I was with him 24 hours a day. I didn't want anyone else taking care of him.

We lived in a little house that my husband's dad and mom owned. It was a really cute little house. I had it fixed up so beautiful and was really proud of it. It had two bedrooms so Chad had his own little room, a living room, dining room, a small kitchen, and a den area that had some crazy orange carpet. I had a real hard time with that, so his dad replaced it with brown carpet. It was close to the airport, so it was a perfect place for us to live for Don's work. We had a great lake up the street that we could walk to, and it was a short drive to see our families, which was very important to me.

One day, while my husband was away on a trip, Chad got sick. He had a bad ear infection. His fever had been as high as 102. I took him to the doctor, and they gave him medication, and the fever went down. Later that night, I got ready for bed. It was still early and not even dark outside, but I was going to lay down with Chad. I had given him his medicine and brought him to my room. I wanted to keep an eye on him, so I laid him in my bed. As I was sitting there on the side of my bed, I felt it shaking. I turned around to see him convulsing. I grabbed him up and as I did, his back arched as he started convulsing in my arms.

I grabbed the phone with my other hand to dial 911. I was screaming into the phone at the operator. She was trying to get my address. As I was talking to her, his eyes rolled back in his head. He stopped convulsing, got stiff, and stopped breathing. I just dropped the phone, ran to the front door and ripped it open, snatching the chain lock off the wall. I ran screaming to my neighbors next door. They came out and grabbed him from me and called 911. By then, help was on its way. When they arrived, they took him, started working on him, and packed him in ice.

When I got to the hospital, they were checking him for brain damage. They didn't know how long he had not been breathing. His fever had climbed to 106, which caused the seizure. I was so afraid. He was about 18 months old when this happened.

The doctors said there could be damage with such a high fever, but everything checked out perfect. He was ok! It was a miracle. I felt so relieved, but at the same time it just made me want to hold on to him even tighter. There was a need in me to keep him safe at all cost. Oh my God, the fear that came upon me to think of anything happening to my child!

I was forever thankful.

Placenta Previa

Two years later, we found ourselves in the middle of a huge project, building our first home. Our dads were builders so we had some great help. My dad was a brick mason and did all the frame and brick work on the home. Don's dad knew all the electricians, painters, cabinet people, and everyone else we needed. It was an absolutely beautiful home. I still love it even today.

My dad did a beautiful arch brickwork in the kitchen. There was an amazing rock fireplace in the den. My parents carried rock up from the creek out back to put in that fireplace. There was also a beautiful antique mantel fireplace with brick inside of it in the master bedroom. I found the mantle in this old antique house and had it refinished. I gave my dad fits while he was designing the arch brick work inside the fireplace, but he did an excellent job. There was nothing my dad couldn't do. There are a lot of special touches of love in that house.

As this house was being built, I got pregnant again. Chad was a little over three then. I was so excited to have another baby on the way. It was definitely time to build a bigger home. We planned the home with three bedrooms. I guess we could have done four, but instead, we made our master bedroom one entire side of the house, and the other two rooms were pretty big. We were all helping with the building of the house. My mom and I sat on buckets and stained all the wooden window frames. She was always a great help and lots of fun. Even little Chad helped out. Sometimes he would get caught on the high scaffolds and get in trouble. He always wanted to be there helping his daddy. It was a beautiful home. I felt so lucky to have such a wonderful place.

Complications

One day while I was over at the new home, (I was always running back and forth over there trying to get things done), I remember being upstairs in the kid's bathroom. We were trying to find some cobalt blue tile for that bathroom. I felt something run down my leg, and I thought maybe I had just had an accident. I wasn't very far long in my pregnancy, only a couple months. I looked down and realized that I was bleeding. I knew this was not a good thing, so I immediately called my doctor, and He told me to come right in.

He determined I had what was called placenta previa (when the placenta covers the opening of the cervix). Mine looked like a possible partial previa, and it was unlikely that I would carry this baby to term. I just sat there at first, not knowing what to say. I never dreamed I would hear this news. I asked him, "What am I supposed to do?" He said, "Absolutely nothing. If you miscarry the baby, you just do." He said there was always a chance that the placenta would correct itself. I just needed to take it easy.

I left the doctor's office that day very upset, thinking that perhaps at any minute of any day, I could lose my baby. I carried that thought with me throughout the entire pregnancy. I was so careful, watching everything I did for fear of having a miscarriage. There is nothing worse than going through a pregnancy with fear. You should have joy while you are pregnant, not fear. My due date was March 28, 1984, and on that morning, I went into labor. I carried my baby full term.

For once, my husband was there when something happened, and we headed over to the hospital. My doctor was there, and needless to say, he was happy to see that this baby had made it to full term. I had some really good doctors, and they really loved what they did. My labor was once again a long one, and my doctor's shift was over, so his partner came in to take over. I would see him in the office from time to time, so we were fine with that. I was not having a good labor. I was having the most horrible labor pain in my back. For some reason, the epidural they gave me did not work, and they couldn't give me another one. So now it was like having a natural delivery.

Anytime someone in our family had a baby, the waiting room would be full. The whole family came and waited. On my husband's side of the family, there had not been a Waits girl in 67 years, so everyone was always excited and hoping for a girl.

When the baby was halfway out, my husband looked at the baby and said, "It looks just like Chad did." Then the doctor said, "You have a baby girl!" I think it took Don a minute to believe it. We were so excited! The first girl in all those years.

When he walked out into that waiting room and announced to our family that we had a baby girl, their reaction was priceless. The look on Chad's face when he saw his baby sister for the first time was priceless. Seeing him hold her was so precious. He was so good with her. It was so wonderful to have a son and now a beautiful baby girl.

Natalie Marie Waits is the name we gave her. We were so blessed to have her. We were blessed with another miracle, another perfect gift from God.

I had gone to the hospital from our old home and returned to our new home with our new baby. How exciting, a new baby and a new home. The family had been moving all our things and getting it all set up before we got home. Our yard was great. There were lots of woods and a creek out back where Chad could play and camp out. It was a great place to grow up. It was all so wonderful. I loved my family, my home, and I loved being a wife and mother.

When Natalie was about eight or nine months old, I woke up not feeling so good. I remember telling Don that I thought I might be pregnant again. I was nursing Natalie, so he didn't think I could be. But we took a pregnancy test, and sure enough, it was positive.

We were not expecting this at all. We thought we had been so careful. The doctor had warned us of the possibility of an incident with placenta previa if I got pregnant again. Well, we were a little shocked, but very excited at the same time. Our family was expanding rapidly.

I had been doing ok for a while, and I was so thankful that things were going well this time. And then one day it happened again, and this time, I panicked. I didn't know what a miscarriage was like, but I was bleeding really bad, and something was falling out of me. I was hysterical! I didn't think I could deal with this again. I got to the doctor's office as fast as I could, and the doctor told me that I had not lost the baby, but I had what they call a full blown previa (the placenta covered the cervix completely). I had lost some placenta and would probably lose more. I was put on bedrest for the remainder of the pregnancy, at least 6 months. They were hoping to get me to the 7th or 8th month. I wasn't allowed to lift anything heavier than the phone. I had to have full time help from both my mother and my mother-in-law. I couldn't even pick up my nine-month old baby girl. She and Chad could sit with me, but I could not go and do things with them like before. I wasn't allowed to travel in case I hemorrhaged, which was a possibility.

There are not many one-story houses in the south, so our home had a lot of stairs. It was a two-story home with a full basement, which had over twenty-two stairs to go down to get to our car. You had to go up at least that many stairs to get to the bedrooms, and there was a deck out back with that many stairs to get to the backyard. There were just stairs everywhere.

My husband made the downstairs living room into a bedroom because I was not allowed to go up the stairs. Everyone took on so much responsibility, everything from cooking, to laundry, to cleaning, and watching the kids. It was incredible, but I felt so helpless watching everyone do everything for me. Every day I would look at a book that showed the development of the fetus by weeks. Every week that went by, I would be so thankful that we had gotten past that week. Because of all the tests they had given me, we knew that we were having another baby boy. I counted every day and every week because every one of them were so critical to his survival.

One evening, everyone had gone to bed. I was so exhausted. It had been a hard week. I had not been feeling good at all and had been losing a lot of placenta and bleeding a lot. The bleeding was hard on my body. It was very painful. It hurt to even walk, and it left me very weak. Four days prior, the doctor had decided to do a test called an amniocentesis. (A long needle inserted into the placenta to remove and test the amniotic fluid) The test involved risks because it was an invasive procedure, but my doctor was very concerned, and he needed to check if the baby's lungs were developed enough to deliver. The test showed they weren't. He needed to stay in as long as I could keep him there.

That night, I had fallen asleep on the couch in our den and had not gone to bed. I woke up feeling like I needed to go to the restroom. I slowly made my way to the bathroom. As I was sitting there, something felt wrong. I looked down and saw blood pouring out of me. I grabbed a towel from the towel rack, put it between my legs, and screamed for my husband. I crawled out the bathroom and into the kitchen. That was as far as I could go. I heard my husband running and falling down the stairs to get to me. He got on the phone and called 911 and his parent and the neighbors to watch our children.

He packed as many towels between my legs as he could to try and stop the bleeding. I was in pure panic. I knew this was it! This was what we had been so careful to avoid, the worst thing that could have happened was happening, I was hemorrhaging. The first thing that came to my mind was that my baby was not going to make it, and my heart was so sad. I had come all this way and had done all that I was supposed to do, and I did not want my baby to die. Then I thought about my son and my little girl and what would happen to them if I didn't make it. I thought about Don and how it was going to be hard for him to have to take care of them by himself. I was so afraid and sad for all of them.

All of these thoughts crossed my mind in a matter of seconds. But then, as all the blood continued to flow out of me, a sudden peace came over me. All the fear just left. I wasn't afraid any more. I stopped thinking about all those things, and I felt complete peace, a feeling that everything was ok. It was like I was floating. I don't remember seeing anything, but I could hear a voice, and something or someone was telling me everything was going to be ok. Somehow, I knew that it would be.

I just remember lying there and hearing people and voices. I believe I was hearing what was going on all around me. I had gone into labor, and was bleeding out on the kitchen floor. The baby would not survive a normal delivery. He would suffocate in the placenta, so they had to get me to the hospital for an emergency C-section to save the baby.

The only thing I can remember is the peace that I felt. I felt like someone was holding my hand, but I was not conscious enough to know if they really were. I thought I heard my husband telling the medics that they could not deliver the baby. It was like he had to keep reminding them.

My husband told me later that there were two doctors, two anesthesiologists, and four nurses waiting for us to arrive. My parents had gotten to the hospital before I arrived in the ambulance. My mom was horrified when she saw me.

Because of the hemorrhaging, the doctors told my husband that I would likely rupture when they delivered the baby. They had to work as fast as they could to help me and to deliver our son. There was no time to wait on anesthesia or blood transfusions, so they began the cesarean without it. I immediately felt a burning pressure, no pain just burning pressure.

The moment our son was born, he was taken to the NICU, the neonatal intensive care unit. We knew that his lungs were not developed. I was not able to see him because they were still working on me. I had lost 8 units of blood, so I was given a blood transfusion. This was back in 1984 when people were getting the HIV virus from blood transfusions. It was a scary time, but I would not have survived without the blood. I later read that there are 8 to 10 pints of blood in the body of an average adult. (https://rrvbc.org) I had nearly bled to death. My doctor said it was truly a miracle that the baby and I survived.

It was a day or two before I saw my son. He was in his little incubator with tubes everywhere, some in his head, his arm, and his feet. He had a tube down his throat for his lungs, so when he cried there was no sound. He was so small, and I was so sad that I was not able to hold him, but I was so grateful that we were alive. I was grateful to see him and touch him and know that he was there, and it was all ok, just like the Presence of Peace told me it would be. We both spent 10 days in the hospital. The doctors were concerned that he may grow up and have issues because of his lungs, but his lungs developed very quickly, and he has had no issues at all. Today, he is in perfect health.

Samuel Ryan Waits was absolutely perfect in every way. God had his hand on him. He was another miracle, another gift from God.

Adjusting to New Things

Being in the hospital for 10 days was probably the best thing that could have happened. In the hospital, they had me on morphine for the pain. When I got home and started moving around, I didn't realize how my body still felt. My mom and mother-in-law came to help. I was so fortunate to have the both of them. I wanted to take care of my children myself, but with a newborn preemie, a 17-month-old, and a 5-year-old, I needed some help. My body just seemed to be in a mess. It had been so long since my body had been "normal." There was no time to stop and let my body complete the healing process. I was emotionally and physically stressed.

I had never had a baby that did not sleep well, but he was up almost every two hours. I ended up having to nurse him and give him formula. After trying about 12, we finally found a formula that he could tolerate. Every time I would hold Samuel to feed him, Natalie would want me to hold her too. So, I had two babies in my arms. She would suck her thumb and rub his head while he ate. So precious! And oh my gosh, what would I have ever done without Chad? He was my little helper. He did everything for me, and he was always happy to do it. He was so good with his sister and brother, and he was so mature for his age. He probably had to do more than he ever should have, but the oldest child always does. As parents, we don't seem to realize how much we are asking of our children at the time.

My body went through so much emotionally and physically that it took me over a year to feel anywhere close to normal again. There were times when I would be emotional and not even know why, but with the passing of time, I got to feeling like myself again.

I was settling into my new life with my three beautiful children. It was absolutely the perfect life for me. I loved being with them every day, just loving on them, taking care of them, and going places with them. Chad went to an amazing school not far away. He loved the school and his teachers, and he excelled in all his classes. He was an amazing, highly intelligent child with a wonderful group of friends. He played baseball, soccer, and was in karate. I wouldn't let him play any football. I was too overprotective. I tried to keep his focus off of that one, which was hard to do because everybody in the south loves football.

There were always kids to play with in the neighborhood, and it was safe. They rode their bikes or big wheels up the street or down the steep drive into the garage. The kids just loved to play outside, and there were just so many fun things to do.

I met a special friend named Linda. Her husband worked for the same man my husband worked for, and we became really close. She was there for me when I needed help the most after the birth of Ryan. She would cook and clean for me and do things that I had never in my life had a friend do. She didn't ask, she just came and did it because she knew the need was there. She is the most amazing woman I have ever met. She even taught me how to smock beautiful dresses for Natalie, and I made lots of them. I even made a Christmas outfit for Ryan one year so he would match Natalie's dress and Chad's outfit. That did not go over so well with their dad, so I didn't make any more boy outfits. I just kept making my girl dresses. I loved dressing Natalie up. She looked like a little princess, and because she was the only little girl on the Waits side, she had jewels too. She was one fancy little girl.

I spent a lot of time alone with my children because my husband's job took him away for long periods of time. He was a pilot for a man who owned his own business.

There were times when he would be gone as long as three weeks. I was so thankful for my friend, Linda, and for being close to my family during those times.

One weekend, my husband was on the deck grilling when Natalie came over to him and laid her arms and hands on the grill. It was a second or two before she even started to scream. It was horrible! We grabbed her and all the kids up, jumped in the car, and drove to the emergency. She never stopped screaming and started going into shock on the way there. The doctors said she had first and second degree burns on her hands and arms and that she would have scars, but she recovered from that trauma and her hands and arms completely healed with no scars, not one sign that it ever even happened.

I knew that there was always going to be scrapes and falls. That was just a part of growing up. But for me, keeping my babies safe was almost an obsession. My husband would want to give them a mile, but I would say no, maybe an inch. It was like they had to always be in my reach so I would know they were safe.

Just knowing the trauma he went through to get here, I was very overprotective of Ryan, especially in the beginning. The fact that his lungs had not been developed when he was born was always in the back of my mind. I was always checking on him to make sure he was breathing ok. I did this for the first year of his life. He was such a small baby. When Ryan turned one on September 8, 1986, he only weighed 19 pounds. The doctor said it takes time for early babies to catch up. I may have been overprotective of him, but that didn't slow him down. He was a very normal, healthy, active little boy, and the older he got, the more he wanted to do everything his big brother did. He was not afraid of anything. He would get on the big wheel at the top of the driveway and go flying down to the bottom and turn sharply into the garage. It would scare me like crazy!

Life was everything I had imagined it to be. Sure, my husband and I had had issues in the past, but we had a family now. This is what marriage and life was supposed to be like. He loved his job, and I loved mine. I thought we had the perfect family!

The Big Move

My husband loved his job, but in his heart, he wanted to fly for the airlines. He got hired by a company that was based out of Phoenix Arizona. So instead of moving the family out, he left for a year and just commuted. This was not easy for any of us. We had only been in our new home less than three years, but commuting was not going to work. In that same year, my grandmother had gotten very ill, so my mom and her sisters had been staying with her full time. I was very close to my grandmother, and I loved her very much.

Chad and I took a trip out to Phoenix to see his dad and visit the area. He wanted us to come and see what we thought about it. I must admit, all I thought was it was drastically different from the south. Where was all the green? From the plane, it looked like another planet. I was not very impressed, but my husband seemed to love it.

After his year there, he was hired by another company that was also based in Phoenix. This was going to be permanent, so he decided to move the family to Phoenix. That was a very hard decision because all our family lived in Alabama. I had lived there all my life, 33 years, and I did not want to leave. It was hard to leave our parents, knowing they would not see their grandchildren as much as they were used to.

I was having to leave everyone and everything I was familiar with. I am a big family person. I love being around my family, having family gatherings and reunions. There was so much joy at those times. I didn't know what I was going to do without all my family, but I knew that my place was with my husband and my family.

I started packing up all of our things. We were going to have to put everything into storage. We had no idea where we were going to live when we got there. My husband had rented us a two-bedroom apartment for the summer until we could find a home, so all the kids packed a few of their special things in their suitcases to bring out to Phoenix. Everything else went into storage. We said our goodbyes to our home, thinking that we would be back someday. My parents drove us to the airport, and with tears in my eyes, I boarded the plane with my three children and headed to Phoenix. It was June 1988.

Chapter 5

When it All Falls Apart

A fter three months of living in an apartment, we found a really nice home in Ahwatukee. It was great for the kids. They each had a room. It was in a cul-de-sac and had a pool, which they loved. We rented some furniture until we could make arrangements to get our furniture out of storage. We had to leave our family pet behind too. She was 15 years old at the time, and I was excited to have her back and be in a home again.

Soon after that, I got a call that my grandmother wasn't going to make it, so I had to make a trip back home. She passed before my flight landed. I was really sad that I was not there to see her. I loved her very much.

After we moved to Phoenix, it seemed that my headaches just continued to get worse. I started to see a doctor out there, and he prescribed me more medication. As months and years went by and the headaches continued to get worse, all he did was increase the medication. He said I was having rebound headaches (headaches caused by the overuse of medication), so he claimed he was going to change my medication. I trusted him and took the new medication, but the headaches never got better. I later found out by my husband's brother, who was a doctor, that my doctor had basically prescribed the same medication under a different name.

I went through years of changing doctors trying to find help for the pain in my head. Some doctors would say it was hereditary because my dad and his mother had headaches and migraines. I even had a doctor ask me if I had children. I said, "Yes, three." He said that was my problem. I did not go back to that doctor. My children were never a problem!

All the doctors that I went to over my 38 years of migraines would tell me that there was no cure for the problem. It was like a shot in the dark to try this or try that. Everything was a new treatment. Everything was a new trial and error. They knew of certain things that could trigger the headaches, but they had no cure.

Some days it would take all my strength to get through a day, especially if my husband was gone on a trip. He was gone three to four days every week. I never had a day without a headache, and some days were worse than others. I knew I had to do my best to function as normal as I could for my children, but it was taking a serious emotional effect on me.

Filling the Void

As the years went by, the migraines increased, and so did the drugs to try to keep them under control. I was looking for answers, but no one seemed to have any. On the outside, I had all that I could ask for. My family was amazing, we had moved into an even bigger house, my husband had his dream job, and I was a stay at home mom taking care of the kids and the home and loving what I did. But why was I in so much pain? There came a point in my life when I had to stop talking about it, or at least I tried to stop. I could tell it was affecting the whole family. If I had to go through this for the rest of my life, this is not going to be good. My medical bills were stacking up. I would still try to do normal things like, exercise, play tennis, and watch the grandkids in the later years, but anything that got the blood pumping would make my head hurt, and I would be done.

I was on so many different narcotics for the severe pain that I would forget things. All the medicine would make me sick, my joints would hurt, and I had even loss lots of weight. I was on Fentanyl, which is more powerful than morphine, methadone, morphine, Botox, Dilaudid, Tramadol, Dihydroergotamine, Imitrex, Topamax, and Seroquel, just to name a few. I took some of these daily. When the migraines would come, they could last up to 6 days. They could come as often as 2 to 4 times a month. It was never-ending.

With everything that was going on in my life, I was sinking deeper and deeper into a dark place. It was hard to explain. How do you explain that you love your husband, your children and what you have, but something is just not right with you? You are missing out on life and so many things because of something that has plagued you all your life. I couldn't put my finger on it, and I was continually looking for help. My husband even suggested I go for psychiatric help, so I went to talk to someone. I found no answers there either. All they wanted to do for me was put me on more medication because they thought I was depressed because I was in so much pain. I just felt like such a victim.

In the late 1990's, my husband got a promotion on his job and was sent to live in Chicago. There was never any talk of us moving there. The kids were all settled in Phoenix. So, there he went commuting again. I only saw him maybe one day a week, if he came home at all. It was for the good of the family. So we could have better things in life, or so he would always say. I just missed having my husband around. I never knew what it was like to not have someone home with me every night. It was like being a single mom. I felt so lonely.

During this time of loneliness, I made a terrible decision. I was unfaithful in my marriage once again. Not like at the beginning of our marriage when I was angry and felt betrayed. This time I was just lonely. I have no other explanation other than something was missing in my heart, and I was looking to fill it. I was lonely and wanted to be loved. I knew it was wrong and selfish on my part. I never wanted to hurt my best friend and the one I loved. I had no idea how horrible the events of my life would become because of what I did. At the hands of my husband, I suffered the most horrific emotional and physical abuse that anyone could ever imagine. No one could have ever told me or made me believe that the man I loved and spent 40 years with was capable of the things that he said and did to me.

Out of respect for my children, I will not go into any details about any of the incidents that occurred over a 15-year period. I see no reason to relive those horrible memories.

Paralyzed by Fear

My husband was so angry about what I had done that he started to emotionally and physically abuse me. I became paralyzed by fear. I never knew if things were going to be ok, or if something would come up, and the abuse would start all over again. I became afraid of the man I had loved for over 30 years. I wanted his love like I always had, but he was hurting me. It was just as I remembered as a child, someone saying they loved me but was hurting me at the same time. I was afraid to be alone with him, afraid to have the door shut when he and I were in the same room, afraid to say something wrong. Fear started to consume me once again.

I was having a really hard time. Love was becoming a horrible thing. In my mind, love was associated with hate, emotional and physical abuse, and control.

Consumed with Shame & Condemnation

The shame I felt for cheating on my husband was so overwhelming. I felt as though I was emotionally falling apart. I was so down and depressed about what was going on in my life. There was no explanation as to why I did it. I was just searching for something I felt I was missing. My husband was my best friend. He had been since I was 17 years old, and he was the last person in the world I would ever want to hurt. But I did, and my heart was hurt, but instead of healing, there was only anger, outrage, retaliation, and abuse.

My marriage was filled with condemnation, pain, and hurt. I don't think I had ever forgotten or forgiven my husband for cheating on me before we were married. Anger and jealousy filled my heart, and I had low self-esteem. After that, I never thought I was good enough. Even though we married and were deeply in love, I could never understand how he could love me, yet I wasn't enough. Why did he have to have so many other women? I was always jealous and suspicious because he was always entertaining other women while I was at home with the kids. Why did he have to always have their attention if he was happy with me? I knew of many pilots who didn't entertain women like he did. Sometime in my thirties, I developed an eating disorder. I was just trying to be in control of something in my life.

One week, we were out of town together when he decided it was a good time to reveal more secrets of infidelity during our marriage. This news was even more devastating, but it should have come as no surprise. It just confirmed all those years of jealousy and suspicion. My biggest mistake that day was not being sympathetic with him. Instead, my heart was hard. I could not understand why I had been abused for doing the exact same thing he was doing. In response, I told him I was elated about what I had done. I paid dearly for those words. That night, he hurt me really bad, and I was afraid for my life. All I could do was cry out to God. I remember hearing him say that I needed to call God to save me.

I held all my children extremely close for fear of anything happening to them. I even put them before my husband. This was probably one of my biggest mistakes. Your husband should always come first. If we went anywhere, the children went too. We rarely took vacations or trips alone. For me, it was all about the children. I just wanted them to be safe. I felt like it was all my responsibility. Nothing was ever going to happen to any of my children. I know that came from never being healed from the loss of my first child.

Everything was out of order.

Things had gotten bad in the later years, and I couldn't protect the children any more. They were getting older, and the things that were going on could not be hidden any longer. My marriage had been a 40-year relationship, and for the most part, I think it had been amazing and wonderful. I married the man I loved, and knew I would be with him for the rest of my life. I adored his family. They were my family for forty years. The purpose of this book is not to condemn a thirty-eight-year marriage. I am just being honest about what went on behind closed doors. It wasn't until the last fifteen years of the marriage that all the ugliness came out. My children grew up in the early years of their lives never seeing or hearing these kinds of things.

I was so ashamed of how it must have made my children feel. I can't even imagine what was going on in their hearts and minds. I took it very personal because my husband knew how protective I was of the kids. The ugly things that were going on, was damaging and just not appropriate for children. We never meant to hurt the kids, but it never got better for them. They were continually being exposed to horrible words, fights, and anything that broke out between the two of us for ten years. We could go weeks, months, and even a year with no issue, then it would happen again. I was always giving in because I wanted so desperately for us to be healed and an answer for all the anger.

Beginning of the End

Things seemed like they were going ok. We had just done some remodeling on our house, and I was really excited about that. I had always wanted a bigger kitchen for our family, so it was going to be so awesome to have a big room for all of us to sit around the dinner table, especially during the holidays, which is my favorite time of the year. It turned out to be a bigger and much more expensive project than we expected. I was hoping to upgrade all the bathrooms and the kitchen, but all we could do was an add-on and the kitchen. It was very beautiful, and I was very proud of how it looked. I loved to decorate my home.

My husband was gone with work all the time, and he was always looking to pick up extra trips on his off days. It had been this way all of his career. Problems started to arise again. I was the instigator, simply because I was so lonely. I was married to a man who loved his work and attention from other women more than me. The screaming and the fighting started again. We never had a normal conversation. There was always screaming, and cursing, and grabbing, and closing me up in a room. The kids would have to come and intervene. My oldest son had to intervene quite a few times. I remember him coming into my daughter's room where I had slept and pulling my husband off of me. He broke through the door. They both nearly went over the balcony.

I can't even imagine what must have been going on in my son's heart and mind at that time. All the yelling and screaming was so frightening for our daughter. She never knew what was going to happen next. I don't even know what our youngest son thought at the time. He seemed to stay silent during it all. There was one incident when my husband had me pinned to a door. He called my youngest son to help him hold me down. I was desperately trying to get away and call 911.

I was not being a good example for my daughter, but I was so hurt emotionally and physically that I felt everything I had done was justified.

One morning, I was coming down the stairs. I remember having something in my hand to talk to my husband about. He was dressed and about to leave for work. I think it had something to do with needing some money, but whatever it was, it triggered something in him. The kids were gone, so it gave him another opportunity to start something with me. He came at me with his fist. He had already broken my jaw a few years back. I fell on the stairs and missed the blow. This time, I immediately made the call to 911. I was done with the physical abuse. The police came as they had over a dozen times over the years. They suggested I get another restraining order. I just wanted some help, and the officers said the courts would help me.

He came back with our youngest son and moved some things out of the house and moved them into our condo. I started receiving messages from him that were too inappropriate to repeat. I never knew anyone could say the hateful things he said to me. It was like he was someone I didn't even know. As always, I took the words to heart. All of it was making me sick and broken. I wanted us to be healed and fixed, but I did not know how. He didn't want help. He just wanted out. He wanted a divorce.

Within two weeks of us separating, he was already dating again, so I honored his request and filed for a divorce. I told the lawyer that I did not want a divorce, but my husband wanted out. I showed him all the horrible emails and threats that he had been sending me. I explained that I was a homemaker, married thirty-seven years with no other source of income. I needed his help? The lawyer said I was doing the right thing.

Spirit of Death

The divorce papers were filed, and the war began. It was the biggest nightmare of my life. I had no idea what I was getting into. It was like what was happening to me was really happening to someone else. There were days when I would wake up thinking that everything was ok and back to normal. I would totally forget that he had left. This actually happened for a few years. I think I was in a state of shock, if that is possible. It was unbelievable to me that the person that I had spent 40 years of my life with could all of a sudden hate me so much. I was worse than a stranger to him. It was like I was an enemy that he was going to the extreme to destroy. I was having a really hard time with this. He had been my best friend for forty years, and my heart was really hurting. I just wanted everything to stop.

The emotional stress was more than I could handle. And then I had the kids who were having a hard time with it as well. They were hurting just as much as I was, and there was nothing I could do to help them at the time. I couldn't even help myself. I just wanted so bad to stop all the terrible things that were tearing our family apart.

After about two months of all the crazy stuff going on with the lawyers, we decided to stop the divorce. I was so excited! For the first time in a long time, I had hope. I believed my prayers were being answered. So, the lawyers wrote up the papers to stop the divorce and sent them to each of us to sign. I signed mine, and then went over to the condo for him to sign, thinking he had to sign the paper I had. I didn't realize he had his own. When I got there, his papers were still sitting on the kitchen table, unsigned. I just looked at him and asked him why hadn't he signed them yet? He said he had changed his mind. He told me he had been dating someone new for about six weeks.

When I asked him how six weeks of dating could compare to thirty-seven years of marriage, he just said I wouldn't understand. He had met her when he lived in Chicago in 1994. So, I actually did understand. This was during the time when he was commuting back and forth to Chicago. He rarely came home. Now I knew why.

Then he decided to try and work things out again. He told me he was breaking things off with his girlfriend. So, while he was still living in our condo, we started seeing each other. But after two months, he admitted that he had still been seeing her. He left on a trip one weekend and sent me a text saying that we were done. So once again, my heart was broken, and my hopes were shattered. The divorce proceedings commenced.

This played out for a year and a half, and the cost was outrageous. The things that were done and said in the courtroom were beyond anything that would come from someone who ever loved you. The pain was horrific. I suffered horrible migraines during the trial and three mini strokes.

I never really completely understood everything that was going on in the courtroom, but I could understand that things were being twisted, and that I had little to say about what was being done. My lawyer was only concerned about himself and ended up leaving me when he realized he wasn't going to get any more money. I had to hire another attorney to finish the trial, which was almost impossible to bring in a lawyer in the middle of a trial.

Through the whole trial, I kept hoping and praying that my husband would wake up and realize how crazy this all was. I just kept praying that he would see how we were letting go of a lifetime of dreams for us and our beautiful family. My heart was breaking for our future and our family's future. Even with all the mess, I knew there was always hope. I couldn't see myself without him. We had always been together. I felt I was losing everything I had ever loved, my husband, my children, everything I had lived for.

I was sick with migraines, scared, and lost. I just didn't want to deal with it anymore. It was way more than I was able to handle. I was familiar with that feeling. I had been down that road before. It became a constant battle in my mind. Now, the darkness had gained strength like I had never known before. The spirit of death that had come on me as a teenager was back again, and it was stronger than anything I have ever had to battle before. I was in a spiritual battle for my life.

Crying out to God

I had totally and completely come to the end of myself. I had no idea what to do anymore. I truly didn't want to go on. I couldn't talk to anyone. Most of my friends couldn't handle being around what was going on.

One morning, in August of 2009, I called a friend named Keo and asked if I could come over. She was someone who would listen and talk to me. We talked, and I told her how hopeless I felt. She said, "Sheila, I want you to go home and start reading your Bible. Start with today's date. On August 10th, read Psalms 10. On August 11th, read Psalms 11, and so on until you read through the Bible." She continued to talk to me about getting back into the Word of God. So, when I got home that day, I did exactly what she said to do. I opened my Bible and began reading the Word of God. I never stopped until I read the whole Bible. I even went and bought a new Bible, The New Living Translation, and I loved it.

As I read the Psalms, my heart began to regain hope. I started to feel good again. I read in the Word that things were going to be good for those who loved the Lord. I had never stopped loving the Lord, but I had turned away from Him. Even though I had turned away from Him, He had never stopped loving me. I realized that because I hadn't had the relationship with the Lord that I needed, I did not truly know love.

I tried to tell my husband that everything would be ok if we put God first in our lives and in our marriage. That was the missing piece that we had been needing. We were married in the church before God. He was the one who joined us together, but we had never made Him first in our marriage or in our family. We never honored His Holy Name like we should have. I could see that this was what we needed to heal. But he wanted nothing to do with it. My heart was crushed. I truly thought he would be so excited at the thought of our marriage being healed and our family being whole. He thought nothing of walking away.

I guess you could say I probably drove him even further away because I would send him scriptures when I would see one that I thought would help him. As I would read through the Bible, I would see something and think, "Yes, he needs to hear that." After about a year, I heard the Lord say, "Are you done now? Now we are going to work on you, Sheila!" And what a work He did!

All Alone

The divorce started in January 2010 and ended in June of 2011. He left in January of 2010 and moved to Chicago with his girlfriend. Our daughter, our son, and granddaughter were living with us at the time. This was a very difficult time for me. Even though we were still married, my husband was acting like we were already divorced. I guess it was just his way of doing everything he could to hurt me. Not long after, my son decided to move away to Austin, Texas.

My daughter and my granddaughter lived with me for about another year. My daughter had gone back to school, and I was helping her with my granddaughter. We were doing the best we could at the house. It was a big house for just us girls. By the beginning of 2011, my daughter had finished school, and she and my granddaughter had decided to move out. Around the same time, the time had come for me to leave the home too. My ex-husband had won the case in court to sell the home.

Once upon a time, I had this big family, and now everyone was gone. I had never been alone before in my life. And here I was all alone in our family home of over 20 years with all of the memories. When it was time for me to leave, there was no one there to help me pack. It was a 4,000-sq. ft. house, and I had no idea where to start. I would come home some days, sit in my garage and just cry out to God and say, "I don't know where to start." But now it was time for me to go. I had hung on to it for too long, hoping that it would somehow keep this family together.

I didn't even know I was divorced. The courts did not send me a divorce decree. I just happened to see a picture of my ex-husband sitting on a park bench with his girlfriend. They were smiling and holding up the divorce decree. The caption on the picture said "When one door closes another door opens." And that's how I found out my marriage of thirty-eight years was over.

I was staying as active as I could in church. I got involved with a women's group that met on the week days, and I joined the choir, which I loved. I have always loved to sing. Some nights, we would do more praying than singing at choir practice. We had a great worship leader.

I needed to stay busy because being home alone was hard. The church that I went to was a big church, and most of the time, I felt alone there, unless I went to a small group activity. I joined a small group of ladies who were on the prayer team at church. They would meet once a week on Monday nights to pray. They were a wonderful, loving group of ladies.

I was so comfortable being married. I did not know how to feel being divorced. I felt ashamed about losing my marriage, and I felt like I was looked down upon. Even though divorce can have the same traumatic effect on your life, people don't tend to comfort you in the same way as they do when you lose a spouse to death. I was not looking for self-pity. I just needed people to understand and not be afraid to talk to me. Loneliness is a killer. It's devastating. Divorce is like a death.

At church, I was as sweet as I could be to the women, but I was not so friendly to men or my friend's husbands. My husband had told me once that men would only give me attention for one reason, and it wasn't my intelligence because I had nothing to say. So, I tried to stay away from the men, so the women would not think I had the wrong intentions. I would act so happy at church and go home so incredibly sad. One time, I took a course at the church on surviving divorce, and even there, I acted like I was already healed and not as bad off as all the others. I was in such denial. I took a course on being abused too. I was doing anything I could to heal all the brokenness inside my heart and mind.

One evening, the church had a program. I can't remember what it was called, but we watched a film and then everyone got into groups and asked questions about God, things we wanted to know and discuss. Later that day, we all got together. The girl that was leading the program said she felt that the Lord was telling her there was someone in the room that had a heart issue and needed prayer. Immediately, I felt she was talking about me because I had been having heart pain. I had gone to the doctor for treatment, had an EKG, and was on medication, but I had never gone up for prayer like that before, so I didn't go.

After the meeting was over, I saw her, and I felt the urge to say something to her. She said she was supposed to pray for me. As she did, I felt heat on my chest. She moved her hand to my back, and the heat went through my body. I started taking deep breaths, which I had not been able to do for weeks. The pain was gone. I just sat there weeping, not really understanding what had happened.

The next morning was Sunday. I woke up really expecting the pain to be back. I was just use to having pain. I took a deep breath, and it was still gone. I just kept breathing, thinking, "Oh my God, it is really gone." When I say the woman who prayed for me at church that morning. I asked her, "What happened to me yesterday? My pain is completely gone. Where did it go?" She just smiled and said, "That was Jesus!" I seriously soaked in that miracle for months.

I met a friend at church name Pat. She and I have become close friends. Pat saw that I was in a lot of pain. She told me about a place called the Healing Rooms. She told me that they met on Tuesdays at a local church and suggested that I go there and get some prayer.

I went that next Tuesday night. It was close to my home, so that was good. When I went inside, I met the sweetest people named Janet and Bob. Then, I was taken into a room and anointed with oil and then they prayed over me. Three different people had a word from the Lord for me. It was the most amazing thing I had ever experienced. I went home that night, opened my Bible and read over all the scriptures that the Lord had given me. I began to meditate on them and the words that the Lord had spoken over me. I felt joy and love like I had never felt before. I couldn't wait to go again. I wanted to hear more of what the Lord had to say. It was the one thing I looked forward to every week. It brought so much healing to my heart and my soul.

Around the same time, my friend Keo invited me to go with her to hear Andrew Wommack, so we went up to the Point South Mountain to hear him speak. He asked anyone who had not been baptized in the Holy Spirit to come up front. Keo said, "Go up there! You need this!" So, I went. He started praying over everybody, and suddenly, the power of God hit me, and words that I have never heard before came flowing out of my mouth. I had no idea what was going on or what had just happened. The whole place was going crazy.

From that day on, it seemed like every time I would start to pray in English, I would start praying in the Spirit. Every time I would sing and worship, I would sing and worship in the Spirit. This opened up a whole new realm to me, a place I had never known before. I began to see things in the Word much differently. I use to read the Word and see things my ex or others had done to me. I had scriptures in my Bible marked for other people. Well, that suddenly changed! Holy Spirit was now taking me to those scriptures to show me things in myself. I was receiving the loving discipline of my Father God.

"For the LORD corrects those he loves, just as a father corrects a child in whom he *delights."* ~ Proverbs 3:12

The Lord had allowed me to come to the end of myself. He had allowed me to be broken so He could heal me and bring me back to who He had created me to be. All I had to do was be open and willing.

"Purify me from my sins, and I will be clean; wash me, and I will be whiter than snow. Oh, give back my joy again; you have broken me- now let me *rejoice."*
~ Psalms 51:7-8

I eventually went through training and started working in the Healing Rooms. What a blessing it was to pray for others and see them be touched by the love of God. Nothing can heal like the love of God, and I was surrounded by people that the love of God was flowing through. It is critical that people who are so wounded feel the touch of God.

I was so thankful to be a part of this family of people in the Healing Rooms who loved the Lord and were passionate about loving people who were hurting. It's always been my passion to love and help others. I found wonderful lifetime friends being connected to that ministry. God ordains our steps for sure.

It was during this time of helping others and loving on others that God began to do even greater works in my life. Just like the pain and the traumas of my life came over time, my healings did not come all at once. Some of the pain just left like a gentle breeze in the night, and all of a sudden, I would notice they were not there anymore. And yet, some left with the violence in which they came.

I never thought I could ever make it through one day without the life that I once had, but I set my face to my Father God. There were times when I would even argue with God about the way things had turned out, but I never turned away from His promise of making things right and restoring my life. My Father had not made the mistakes in my life, I had. No matter what struggle I was going through, I could see His love and grace in the mist of it all.

Chapter 6

Encounters with God

I had opened the door for a spirit of death to come in when I made the decision to take a drug overdose at eighteen years old. I was not mature enough and definitely not strong enough in the Lord to know who I was in Him. I put all my worth in a man, and when he failed me, that was the only way I saw out. I wasn't usually a depressed person, but towards the end of my marriage and during the worst of the abuse, suicidal thoughts were always there. Combined with all the migraines, I was in a dark and ugly place, and it was real.

There was a powerful feeling that would come over me and it was constantly pulling me to a place of nonexistence. I don't really have the words to explain it, but I don't think the enemy cares how long it takes to get you there. He comes into your life little by little and subtly takes bits and pieces, and before you know it, you are completely broken. The Bible says he prowls around like a lion, ready to devour his prey. When I think of a lion, I think of him sneaking up on his prey.

I was in this dark place many times, and the only thing that kept me hanging on was the thought of my children. I loved them so much. I had already hurt them with other decisions I had made, and I did not want to cause them any more pain. It was hard to talk about and ask for prayer for a lot of the things I was going through, but God always seemed to bring the right person into my life at exactly the right time.

Jesus Rescued Me

In 2010, the Lord started coming to me in dreams and visions and through other people to give me guidance and direction. On one evening, I was having one of my not so good days. Anyone who has gone through any serious trauma can tell you, you can be feeling great one minute and feel like the world is crashing the next. Sometimes I could not get off the floor or leave the house. Well, this was one of those nights. I can't remember if I had dozed off and had a dream or if it was a vision, but I saw myself under water. I was in the deep ocean with dark, black water. I could not see a thing because I was so far under the water, and I knew that I was drowning. I was struggling and trying to breathe, and I remember reaching up with my hand and crying out to God.

When I did, I instantly felt the hand of God pull me out of the water and rescue me. I remember taking this great big breath of air. I came out of the darkness into the light. Out of death and into life. Though the enemy tried to keep me bound, he could not. The love of my Father God rescued me.

I didn't realize it at the time, but what God was showing me in this dream or vision was the enemy was trying to keep all the traumas, abuse, pain, and everything that had happened in my life hidden in the deep, dark waters. You see, if he can keep them hidden from us, we will continue to be sick. The enemy wants to keep the body of Christ sick and ashamed, but God wants what is hidden to come out of the dark waters and be exposed. Then the Light of Christ Jesus can start to heal the broken places.

I am reminded in scriptures of Psalms 18. It is exactly how I envision the Lord.

"The ropes of death entangled me; floods of destruction swept over me. The grave wrapped its ropes around me; death laid a trap in my path. But in my distress I cried out to the LORD; yes, I prayed to my God for help. He heard me from his sanctuary; my cry to him reached his *ears."* ~ Psalms 18:4-6

"He reached down from heaven and rescued me; he drew me out of deep waters. He rescued me from my powerful enemies, from those who hated me and were too strong for me. They attacked me at a moment when I was in distress, but the LORD supported me. He led me to a place of safety; he rescued me because he delights in *me."* ~ Psalms 18:16-19

This was the first vision or dream that I can vividly recall of the Lord coming to deliver me out of the darkness that I was in. It has stayed with me ever since it happened. It was real. When you have an encounter with the Lord, something in you changes. You are never the same again.

As I was praying in the Spirit one day, I saw stairs. As I started moving down the stairs, I could see old stone, like you would see in a dungeon. I have never been in a dungeon, but it looked like something I had seen in movies. I felt really sad. There was something about that place. There was no feeling of life there. I kept going, and I saw what looked like a cell and someone in a fetal position lying on a bed facing a wall. As I got closer to the person, I realized it was me. I just stood there looking down at myself. I was lifeless and had no strength. There was nothing I could do or say to help me.

Then I looked to the side of me, and I saw Jesus coming down the stairs with a key to open the door. He opened the door, came over, and picked me up off the bed, and carried me up the stairs into the light.

Then I woke up! My spirit had been locked up in a prison for so long that only Jesus could set me free. Jesus is our Freedom! Jesus is our Healer!

Let Jesus carry you out of the prison that you may be locked up in. Let Him carry you out of the deepest, darkest places where no one else can go or can get to. His love is higher and deeper than anything you can imagine.

Tunnel Vision

One night, at a home schooling for Bethel School of Supernatural Ministry, we had two guests. One was the author of a book of decrees from Psalms. I bought the book, and she autographed it and wrote something in it for me, but I didn't have time to look at it before we started our meeting. After the meeting was over, I talked with our other guest, who was a prophet from Germany for a while and then went on home. When I got home, I remembered Beth had written in my book. She had given me a message that she said the Lord had given her for me. It was one of the decrees from her book "Light and Way" and was signed, "Blessings, Beth." So, I turned to the page in her book and began to read all the blessings over my life.

The next morning, I got a call from my friend, Janet, who had hosted the meeting the night before. She said the guest from Germany had had a vision about me, but the timing was not right for him to share it. She said she would call me later that day for him to talk to me. She called about 5:30, and he got on the phone. He began to tell me his vision. He said he saw me in a car - in a dark tunnel. I was driving at a high rate of speed.

I was trying to get out as I saw a glimpse of light (sunlight) ahead. I was following the light. Suddenly, there was a huge brick wall right in front of me. I only had two choices — crash or hit the brakes. I hit the brakes and stopped right in front of the wall. I got out of the car and saw Jesus standing there. He took me by the hand and led me out of the dark tunnel.

I knew in this vision the Lord was telling me that my life had been on a fast track to a dead end, and I had only a split second to make a decision on how I wanted it to continue. It was comforting to me to know that Jesus was there helping me out of that dark place.

I got two words from the Lord that night, a vision and the words "Light and Way" with the scripture Job 22:28. This is what the Lord spoke to me.

"You will succeed in whatever you choose to do, and light will shine on the road ahead of *you."* ~ Job 22:28

Jesus is the Light that will always shine on the road ahead of me.

Jesus Reveals Himself to Me

I was in my bathroom one morning getting dressed. I was singing and praying. I find that's a fun way to get dressed. Lots of times, I like to just pray in the Spirit, and this was one of those days. As I was praying, I suddenly found myself back in that framed house in my old neighborhood where I had been molested. I saw myself calling for my brother and sister. I remember being there and being afraid of being alone. Suddenly, I realized Jesus was there with me. I felt safe from what could have been, and suddenly, I wasn't afraid anymore. It was the strangest feeling. I felt like I was there, and I wasn't afraid any more. When I came back out of this vision, I was weeping, but I felt a weight had been lifted off of me. Jesus had been there and protected me from far more than I knew of. I felt a breaking off of the spirit of the fear of man that had been on me since I was a little girl. I felt so incredibly free.

Deliverance

The Lord was doing a major healing in me, but He was doing it little by little. I believe there was so much that needed healing. The trauma of losing my child was the hardest. I had never gotten over losing my first child, and I constantly wondered how things could have been different. I would always look at my other children and know exactly how their sibling would have looked because they were all so much alike, so amazing and so beautiful.

Losing a baby, regardless of how or why, is one of the most painful things in the world to experience. A piece of you is missing, and it's never recovered. I never got to see or hold my baby, but he was a gift from God, and he was loved. I have loved and missed him for 42 years.

One day I began to pray in the Spirit, asking God for forgiveness for letting go of my child. As I began to pray, I felt the presence of the Holy Spirit come upon me, and I went into deep, violent prayer. There is no other way to explain what happened. The violent prayer went on for a long time. I started throwing up. When it ended, I was completely exhausted. This is when I realized that the Lord was taking me back to the time of when it happened and delivering me from the trauma of losing my child. I was reliving the whole incident all over again, but He was healing the pain and the loss.

This was a revelation and a beginning of helping me overcome the brokenness that I had lived with all my life. I had been praying and asking the Lord to search the deepest places of my heart, for only He knew the depths of my pain. I was willing to do whatever it took to be free. Sometimes the healing process is not pretty. Opening up old wounds and going down deep into the root of the pain is very painful, but I knew that my Father God's love for me was perfect, and it was the only thing that was going to heal me. My garden was full of weeds, and He was pulling them up by the roots. I needed a relationship with my Father again, so we could walk together in the cool breeze of the garden.

It was what my heart so desperately wanted.

Chapter 7

The Amazing Cross

I truly believe that it will take all eternity to grasp all that God the Father did through Christ Jesus on the Cross. There has never been and never will be such a demonstration of relentless love. Once God got a hold of my heart through His Word by speaking to me about the love Jesus poured out on the cross that day, He wrecked my life.

Even though I had grown up in a loving family, fell in love and married as a young girl, I had truly never known love. For the first time in my life, even though I had been baptized at 10, I was personally meeting the God who was and is Love.

The cross was where it all began. It was where His ultimate love was poured out for me so that I might live again. Jesus was revealing to me just how much my Father loved me by dying on the cross for me. He paid the ultimate price for all my sins so I would never be punished for them and live a life of freedom. This was one of the greatest revelations I have ever had. I had freedom! He chose me long ago, before I was ever born into this world, He knew everything about me from beginning to end, and He created me to be free in Him.

I understood that His mercy and His grace was nothing that I deserved. It's just who our Father is. There is absolutely no one like Him. He loves us so incredibly much that all He wants to do is bless us with amazing lives. Just think about how much you want to give good things to your own children. I can't think of anything I wouldn't do for my children. I love to buy them gifts. There is nothing more enjoyable. Well, your Father in Heaven wants to give you more than you could ever imagine.

"For God in all his fullness was pleased to live in Christ, and through him God reconciled everything to *himself."* ~ Colossians 1:19-20

When Jesus, the spotless Lamb of God, went to the cross for me and for you and cried out, "It Is Finished," His work here on earth was done. It was then up to us to receive this amazing gift of grace for complete healing—spirit, soul, and body. This is the gift we have here now to live and abide in.

"Yet it was our weaknesses he carried; it was our sorrows that weighted him down. And we thought his troubles were a punishment from God, a punishment for his own sins! But he was pierced for our rebellion, crushed for our sins. He was beaten so we could be whole. He was whipped so we could be healed. All of us, like sheep, have strayed away. We have left *God's* paths to follow our own. Yet the LORD laid on him the sins of us *all."* ~ Isaiah 53:4-6

Agape Love

"Jesus Christ is the same yesterday, today, and *forever."* ~ Hebrews 13:8

The love of God is perfect. He is perfect love. The same love He had when He created man in the garden is the same love He has today. The same love He had when He sent Jesus to give His life on the cross is the same love He has today. His love will never change.

Knowing how much our Father loves us and receiving His love is so important. Love is the key to our relationship with Him. There should not be any roadblocks in the way of receiving the love of your Father.

Just imagine yourself as a parent and how much you love your own child, yet, they can't seem to grasp the depth of your love for them! Can you imagine how your heart would feel? When I could not receive my Father's love for things I had done, I started seeing it in this way. There was a time when all I wanted to do was love my children, but there was no love in return. I knew what the pain of that was like, so I decided at that moment that I would never not receive love from my Abba Father! I can't even begin to list the wonderful things He has done for me in my life. But the one most important thing is, I am with Him now. I am back in my Father's house where I belong. I know who I am. I am His daughter. I am so loved by Him, and nothing and no one can take that away from me. It's my greatest miracle.

"*I* pray that from his glorious, unlimited resources he will empower you with inner strength through his Spirit. Then Christ will make his home in your hearts as you trust in him. Your roots will grow down into *God's* love and keep you strong. And may you have the power to understand, as all *God's* people should, how wide, how long, how high, and how deep his love is. May you experience the love of Christ, though it is too great to understand fully. Then you will be made complete with all the fullness of life and power that comes from God." ~ Ephesians 3:16-19

Without His love, we are truly not living a life of abundance. His love is what makes us complete. It is the love that was created in us. When we are filled with His love, we have the ability to give love, the kind of love that He came and set the example for us to follow. Once we freely receive this love, we are able to freely give because it never runs out.

"Three things will last forever - faith, hope, and love - and the greatest of these is *love.*" ~ Corinthians 13:13

Forgiving Myself

The process of forgiving myself was the absolute hardest road for me. The absolute hardest! Even though I had asked for forgiveness, I continued to feel guilty for decisions that I had made in my life. I wonder if this is why Jesus said to Mary when she saw Him at the tomb, "Go and tell all my disciples, including Peter, that I have risen." I think Jesus knew Peter would have a hard time forgiving himself.

My heart was filled with anger, fear, and, unforgivness towards myself. I had so much regret for the loss of my child that it led to guilt, and that guilt led to fear. I lived in fear of everything. Fear of what might have been and even of what I might lose. I battled with this for a long time after coming back to the Lord, but He is such a patient, loving, and kind Father. He is never in a hurry. His love just remained strong and mighty for me until I got the full understanding of His grace and mercy. I just continued to let Him teach me about His love and pour His love out on me, which completely changed what I thought about myself.

It is a must that you forgive yourself. All the blessings of your Heavenly Father will fill you and flow through you. I wake up every day and thank my Heavenly Father for His grace and His mercy!

I had been really praying and seeking the Lord as to why it was so hard for me to let go of the guilt. He revealed to me that it was a heart issue. I was believing what Jesus had done for me on the cross. I had confessed my sins and repented, but when it came to the issue of my child, I was not receiving God's forgiveness in my heart.

I had what is called pseudo guilt. It comes when you confess your sins, but you don't really feel forgiven.

This was not pleasing to God because He had already forgiven me by sending His Son to die for me on the Cross. So, if I continued to dwell on the issue and let it torment me, I was not really believing what Jesus did for me on the Cross.

This just brought me to a complete stand still when I realized this. God had already punished Jesus for all I had done and will do. But instead of accepting what He had done for me, I thought I could do a better job of punishing myself!

Fear was one of the main reasons I couldn't forgive myself. I had not been made perfect in His LOVE - for fear is associated with punishment.

Oh my gosh, what a revelation! The enemy had had his way with me for nearly my entire life. It was time to say, "NO MORE."

"Such love has no fear, because perfect love expels all fear. If we are afraid, it is for fear of punishment, and this shows that we have not fully experienced his perfect *love.*" ~ 1 John 4:18

He Restores my Soul

"*Haven't* you read the scriptures?" Jesus replied. "They record that from the beginning '*God* made them male and *female.*' And he said, "This explains why a man leaves his father and mother and is joined to his wife, and the two are united into one.' Since they are no longer two but one, let no one split apart what God has joined *together."* ~ Matthew 19:4-6

Having your marriage come to an end is more than a break. It's a rip and a tear in the heart. No one can understand the damage that it does to you. Even those individuals that are going through it themselves each have their own valleys to go through. I cannot fathom anyone going through this trial without the grace of God.

All through my marriage of almost thirty-eight years, I was someone who professed to be a Christian. I was baptized at ten, went to church occasionally, loved my husband, my family, and people. I was a good person, but I was not a Christian by God's standards. And I am not talking about rules. I am talking about the Jesus that I have come to know. The Savior of the world that came to Earth to show us how to live in love for one another, how to care and respect one another, how to teach our children the amazing and wonderful love and goodness of our Father, how to love ourselves and know who we are as children of the Most High God, so we walk in this world with grace and confidence and never have fear of what man thinks about us.

I ran straight into the arms of God before I had to go through this battle. This was one battle I knew He was definitely going to have to fight for me. No matter what the outcome, I knew my God was still in control. He knows the beginning and the end. He knows the heart of all concerned, and He knows what is best. I knew all things would work out according to His purpose in Christ Jesus.

I went to the Healing Rooms to get prayer for myself on 11/11 (I love these numbers). This was right after the divorce. Pastor Mike, from Love Gospel, prayed for me and gave me these words from the Lord. They are still in my Bible today, and I meditate on them all the time.

"Comfort for Your Soul" ~ Psalms 23
"Strong and Courageous, do not be afraid, for He is with you." ~ Joshua 1:9
"As your soul prospers" ~ 3 John 2
"Called to a higher place" ~ Revelation 4:1-2

The Lord told me if I wanted complete healing, it was going to start in my soul. When you stop trying to fight the battle and let Him do the fighting by just releasing yourself into His hands and letting Him have His way with you, He will heal your wounded soul. As your soul begins to prosper, your life will flourish and live again. You will come to that place of rest in Him and live out of that place. I love where it says in Psalms 23, "You lead me beside the still waters, you restore my soul." That is such a healing place for me.

What I would like to say to anyone who may be going through such a heartbreak is don't let anyone put you on a time limit for getting over your loss. It will happen in God's timing. I personally don't believe time heals. I believe only God can heal the brokenhearted. Trust Him. Let Him love you and guide you through the valleys and the mountains. Let God restore the years to cause everything to turn out for good.

Giving it All to God

"Give all your worries and cares to God, for He cares about *you."* ~ 1 Peter 5:7

Isn't it amazing that our father God wants us to give all of our worries and cares to Him? I just find that so awesome. Our Abba God wants to take every and anything that is hindering us off our plate. He is such a good, good Father.

If we could only understand the magnitude of His goodness, our feet would never touch the ground!

I am learning in my walk with the Lord that if anything from my past hurts me, or something I'm feeling is not of the Lord, I just immediately give it to Him. If there is a thought in my mind that I feel is not ok, I give it to Him. I am making this a good habit of mine, and it's amazing how you can change habits pretty fast. I want nothing to do with anything that may offend me. It's something we have to choose to do.

I think He wants us to give everything to Him. When you go to Him to tell Him about your cares, just spend some time with Him. Don't you love spending time with your earthly father. Your Heavenly Father is just longing to spend time with you, to listen to your voice, to hear what You have to say. He already knows everything you are going to say anyway; He just wants to hear it from you.

"*You* know what I am going to say even before I say it, LORD" ~ Psalms 139:4

Forgiving Others

"*If* you forgive those who sin against you, your heavenly Father will forgive you. But if you refuse to forgive others, your Father will not forgive your *sins.*"
~ Matthew 6:14-15

This Word of God may seem hard for some to understand, but how can we come to the cross with all our sin and ask for forgiveness and not be forgiving in return. I hear stories all the time from people that just flat out say that there is no way they would ever be able to forgive someone for what they did to them. I completely understand! I have been in that situation, hurt so deeply by a loved one that its beyond your understanding. But what you need to understand is forgiveness does not make what the person did to you right. You are choosing not to hold what they did against them by giving it to the Lord. The Lord tells us in His Word that we are to pray for those who have hurt us.

All I can tell you is this, when you have truly received forgiveness and know you have been redeemed by the blood of Christ Jesus, you cannot help but give that same forgiveness to others. There is something in your heart that wants others to have and know what you have received. I don't care what they have done to you, you just want them to have it too. Every good thing you pray for in your life, you should pray for others to have it in theirs also.

"*You* have heard the law that says, '*Love* your *neighbor*' and hate your enemy. But I say, love your enemies! Pray for those who persecute you! In that way, you will be acting as true children of your Father in heaven. For he gives his sunlight to both the evil and the good, and he sends rain on the just and the unjust alike. If you love only those who love you, what reward is there for that? Even corrupt tax collectors do that much. If you are kind only to your friends, how are you different from anyone else? Even pagans do that. But you are to be perfect, even as your Father in heaven is perfect." ~ Matthew 5:43-48

Forgiveness is a decision of your will. You cannot rely on your feelings because they can never be trusted. Your feelings and emotions will more than likely never lead you to forgiveness. Since God commands us to forgive, it's a choice that we should all make. It's a decision that you must make over and over again and continue to give it to the Lord until you have received the grace of God to forgive. The offender may not ever want forgiveness and may never change, and that can be very hard to accept, but that doesn't change the way God wants us to react. We are to always have a forgiving spirit, no matter what. Forgiveness can for sure be painful, but it is what God has called us to do, and it is for our good. He is our Father who knows so much more than we do. He truly knows what is going to be best for us. As we continue to give everything to Jesus, He will cause our emotions to line up with His.

The beauty of forgiveness is that it sets us free. It is given to us by our loving Father for our good and for His Glory.

God's Love

"*We* love each other because he loved us *first*" ~ 1 John 4:19

"We know how much God loves us, and we have put our trust in his love. God is love, and all who live in love live in God, and God lives in *them.*" ~ 1 John 4:16

Love is the essential key to a relationship with God and our relationship with others. It is in His love and by His love that we are capable of loving others. God enables us to love Him and to love others by first receiving His love. We must learn how to come to our Father as little children and receive from Him. There is just no way any of us can know how to help one another and make a difference in a hurting world unless we come and be filled with His love.

Because of Jesus' sacrifice for me on the cross, His Blood has allowed me to go right into the throne room of Heaven with boldness before my Abba Father and receive a continuing overflow of His love. It's a river that comes from the throne of God, and it never ends. I can swim in this river and go to the deepest depths and be filled with His love. There is just no end to the presence of His love.

When you come into the presence of the Lord God, you can simply empty out all of your junk and everything old and not of Him. You will be filled with supernatural love, because He is Love. His power and presence will take its place in your life. The Holy Spirit will be able to do the work in you that He has been longing to do.

I Praise God for the Holy Spirit! What would we ever do without our Comforter and Friend. I was thinking one day about how it must have been when everyone was trying to get to Jesus, to hear Him speak, to have Him pray for them and heal them. Could you imagine if we all had to go to one place to see Jesus to get prayer and healing today! Oh my goodness!

I absolutely love Holy Spirit; He is the love of my life. I am so thankful my Father God loved me so much that He sent me someone who would be my closest friend ever, someone who would never ever leave my side, and someone who would always lead me in the right direction. He loves me with pure passion. He protects me from any harm in my life. I know He is with me all the time.

It's one thing for someone to give you a gift, but it's a whole different feeling to receive a gift. When you receive a gift, you are retrieving something. It doesn't just lie there dormant anymore. It has an impact on your life. When you receive this gift of love from God, the impact is life changing. I call it "Transformation," and God has truly transformed my life. This is what God is doing in the Body of Christ today. He is transforming His people back into what He created them to be in Christ Jesus.

"This is real love - not that we loved God, but that he loved us and sent his Son as a sacrifice to take away our *sins."* ~ 1 John 4:10

Amazing Grace

"All praise to God, the Father of our LORD Jesus Christ, who has blessed us with every spiritual blessing in the heavenly realms because we are united with Christ. Even before he made the world, God loved us and chose us in Christ to be holy and without fault in his eyes. God decided in advance to adopt us into his own family by bringing us to himself through Jesus Christ. This is what he wanted to do, and it gave him great pleasure. So we praise God for the glorious grace he has poured out on us who belong to his dear Son. He is so rich in kindness and grace that he purchased our freedom with the blood of his Son and forgave our sins. He has showered his kindness on us, along with all wisdom and understanding. God has now revealed to us his mysterious plan regarding Christ, a plan to fulfill his own good pleasure. And this is the plan: At the right time he will bring everything together under the authority of Christ - everything in heaven and on *earth."* ~ Ephesians 1:3-10

There is not a day that I don't thank Him for this amazing gift, this greatest gift of grace and the mercy of His Son Jesus Christ on the Cross. I will probably never fully know the magnitude of it until I see my Heavenly Father. Its undeserved, unmerited grace. There is no greater gift of love. He has given me so much, and all He wants from me is to continue to receive it. It gives our Father such pleasure to have us come and receive more of His goodness and blessings all the days of our lives. This is the way we are to live and dwell in His house, in His glory on this earth. This is living in freedom, the freedom that Jesus gave so much for. He gave His life for this freedom. Freedom in Christ!

"Furthermore, because we are united with Christ, we have received an inheritance from God, for he chose us in advance, and he makes everything work out according to his *plan."* ~ Ephesians 1:11

How much more could we possibly ask for? We are God's children, and the Kingdom of God is our home, our inheritance. We are sons and daughters of the Most High God. We are royalty. This has been our Father's plan all along, that we were to live in this place of Heaven here on earth. The garden was perfect. It was lacking nothing, even we were lacking nothing. The Lord was always there, and we had all we needed.

"And now you Gentiles have also heard the truth, the Good News that God saves you. And when you believed in Christ, he identified you as his own by giving you the Holy Spirit, whom he promised long ago.

The Spirit is *God's* guarantee that he will give us the inheritance he promised and that he has purchased us to be his own people. He did this so we would praise and glorify *him."* ~ Ephesians 1:13-14

So, you see, this is God's promise to me and to you. When Jesus ascended to Heaven, we now have the Spirit of God. Holy Spirit is our promise and our guarantee that we have received an inheritance from God.

We can rest in this truth; God has a perfect plan and nothing in Heaven and earth or below the earth will interfere with His plan. He is still in control. I am so thankful that He loves me and loves to partner with me and you to do great things for the Kingdom. But most of all, I Honor His Holy Name, for He is Worthy. He is the All Powerful One. The Great I AM!

Chapter 8

Finding Peace

As lonely as I was, I never thought I would ever find peace. But one day as I was reading the Word of the Lord, He spoke to me through a scripture, and it became my all-time favorite. I wrote it on a piece of paper and put it on my refrigerator and read it every day. I let it sink into my heart as I would repeat it over and over. I still do all the time.

"Seek the Kingdom of God above all else, and live righteously, and he will give you everything you *need."*
~ Matthew 6:33

The Lord was telling me to put Him first, not what I was missing and sad about. The Lord was taking me through a healing process, but this word was so powerful. I was so focused on what I had lost, I was not allowing Holy Spirit to do a complete work in me. I was not willing to let go. My thoughts were of me, my sadness, my loss, and not The Lord.

When I got this revelation in my heart, I began to focus my eyes on Jesus. I truly began to put Him first in my thoughts and in my words. When any sad feelings would try to invade my mind, I would immediately begin to talk to Holy Spirit, and I would repeat the Word of

God. There is so much power in God's Word! I would purposely choose to put the Kingdom of God before all my issues because He says to put Him first, then anything I needed will be added unto me. This completely changed my life. It changed my whole thought pattern, my dreams at night, and completely changed my world.

Because I have put Him first, if I need peace, He gives me peace. If I need joy, He brings me joy. If I need help, He always meets the need. Even if your need is not met immediately, believe that it has been met, contend for it, and wait on the Lord to bring it to manifestation. He tells us not to worry about all the things of the world, for look at all the beauty in the world. Look at the flowers in the field and the birds He feeds. Why do we have so little faith? Aren't we more precious to Him than the birds? We are His most precious possession. There is nothing He will not do for us.

I think this scripture is like the Rock of Jesus. It's like the foundation of who He is. If your life is not in this order, you will not have a solid foundation. He is the beginning, so you must seek Him first. He is all things and all things are of Him. If you seek after Him, His character (all of who He is), you will lack nothing.

Revelation

"*Then* as I looked, I saw a door standing open in heaven, and the same voice I had heard before spoke to me like a trumpet blast. The voice said, "*Come* up here, and I will show you what must happen after *this.*" And instantly I was in the Spirit, and I saw a throne in heaven and someone sitting on *it.*" ~ Revelation 4:1-2

When the Lord gave me this word on 11-11, I prayed about it, but I was so focused on being caught up in the Heavens, it took me a while to understand what the Lord was saying to me.

Jesus is the doorway. He was calling me to come up to where He was and look at my situation from His view. He wanted me to see that my Father God was still seated on His throne, and He was still very much in control of my life. Nothing that had gone on or happened in my life had taken Him by surprise. He already knew every detail before I did.

Now, I worship and praise the Lord and go up into the Heavens all the time. I have learned that this is what the Lord was wanting me to do. To live above my earthly circumstances and see things from my Heavenly perspective.

I am His precious daughter. He has a special interest in everything that I am doing in my life. There is nothing I can't come up into the Heavens and ask Him about. There is nothing He won't help me with or give me if it is for my good.

I would say about ninety percent of the time, I just say "Lord, show me what you want me to see." Receiving from Him rather than asking Him for something is the best times for me.

The Lord is looking for all His children to understand who they are as Kingdom sons and daughters. He is looking for all of us to come up there, into the Heavenly realm, to pray, decree, and live out of this realm. Everything that you need to know and see is there with Christ Jesus.

Comfort for My Soul

"The LORD is my shepherd; I have all that I need. He lets me rest in green meadows; he leads me beside peaceful streams. He renews my strength. He guides me along right paths, bringing honor to his *name."*
~ Psalms 23:1-3

One of the words that I received from the Lord on 11-11 was "comfort for your soul."

I can't tell you how many times I have said these words either out loud or whispered them in my mind. I would go on walks and would repeat that the Lord is my shepherd, and I have all that I need. He has led me beside the still waters, and He has restored my soul.
I read once about how sheep totally depend on the shepherd for everything. The shepherd must protect them, provide for them, and guide them everywhere they go. Even though we are not helpless like sheep, we do have the wisdom to choose to follow the Good Shepherd who says in His Word that He will lead us to green pastures and peaceful streams. He knows where the green pastures and the peaceful streams are. He is the creator of all things.

I don't know about you, but when I was living in the ways of this world and thinking that I was living the good life, my life was spiraling out of control more than I even knew it was. My eyes were so blind to my rebellion; I could not see the serious damage I was doing to myself or those around me. When we chose to rebel against God and turn our backs on all the blessings and goodness He has offered us, we cannot blame God for the mess we create.

He is the Good Shepherd, and He is always standing at your door and knocking to come in. It's not that you can't hear Him knocking, the question is, are you going to let Him in? You have to open the door from your side. Every second of every day you can make that choice. The Lord says:

"*Seek* the LORD while you can find him. Call on him now while he is *near.*" ~ Isaiah 55:6

We are living in a world where the Body of Christ is so depleted, and this is not the plan of The Lord. He is restoring His people, and it starts in the soul. God provides us with His Word, the means of giving us spiritual nourishment, rest in Him, and restoration for our souls.

When David spoke of the Lord as his shepherd, he was saying He was his provider, his protector, and also his King.

The King of Kings and Lord of Lords is the only one that can give you peace and heal your soul. He is peace, and the more time you spend with Him, the more your heart will change and your soul will heal. He touches you in the deepest of places that only He can touch. When you get to the place of rest in Him, this is where you stay. This is where you abide. This is the green meadow.

It's critical that we pay attention to the words of the Lord when He speaks about the healing of our souls. The Lord spoke to me about it in so many ways, and the instant I took hold of His Word and began to receive the healing I needed, I received healing and miracles. Another word the Lord gave me on 11-11 was "as your soul prospers."

"Dear friend, I hope all is well with you and that you are as healthy in body as you are strong in *spirit."* ~ 3 John 2

This is the word the Lord gave me, and when my soul began to heal, I began to receive physical healings. This is what the Lord has given everyone, all of His people, the freedom to be free of all their soul wounds and to be in perfect health.

Lord, we thank you for taking away our wounds and replacing them with Your peace and Your rest. There is no one like You, there is nothing like Your love.

God's Word

I will never forget when I came back to the Word of God in the summer of 2009. I had an old family Bible, and I was having a hard time understanding it. So, I immediately got a recommendation from a friend for a good Bible that I could understand. It had been so long since I had been in the Word. I was so excited, and I loved my new Bible. I was reading the Word every day and have not stopped since then. It's not something I feel I have to do, it's something I love to do. It's something I can't get enough of. I even read the Bible from the beginning to the end. I think I read it in 90 days. It was the most amazing thing I had ever done. I had the most amazing awakening of who my Father was, when I read from the beginning to the end.

I had such passion in my heart for my Father God. The power of His Word opened my eyes and my heart to the passion and mercy of our Father for all of His children. I had grown up and never knew our Father God in this way. I knew him as the God who judges. How did I attend church and not know who my Father was? If anyone has not read straight through the Word of God, I would highly suggest you do.

Everything and anything that you need in your life can be found in the Word of God. When I was in the deepest, darkest place in my life, the Word of God brought life into my life. Every question I had, there was an answer, and for every sorrow, there was hope. When I was sad, I would find joy. Reading the Word of God was changing everything about the natural way of my life. For the Lord says:

"For you have been born again, but not to a life that will quickly end. Your new life will last forever because it comes from the eternal, living word of *God."* ~ 1 Peter 1:23

Everything that the Lord had to show me was right there in His Word. Where I needed change in my life, where I had made wrong decisions, it was all there. It was like looking at myself in a mirror, and it was not a pretty picture. Healing and discipline is never pretty, but it was so necessary.

Even though it's not an easy process, I will tell you what worked best for me. I just humbled myself before the Lord. Anything and everything that the Holy Spirit would bring up, I would repent and ask for forgiveness. Let the power of God's Word heal you. For the Lord says:

"For the word of God is alive and powerful. It is sharper than the sharpest two-edged sword, cutting between soul and spirit , between joint and marrow. It exposes our innermost thoughts and *desires."* ~ Hebrews 4:12

Worship and Praise

"Yet you are holy, enthroned on the praises of *Israel."* ~ Psalms 22:3

The Word of God says that our Father inhabits the praises of His people. How marvelous and exciting to know that He dwells and lives in that atmosphere of our worship and praise. When we love on Him and give Him the honor that He so deserves, the glory comes down. Oh my Lord, there is no other place I would rather be than in the glory of the Lord. When His Glory comes down, the power of His presence comes down. Oh, how I love His presence and His Glory. I want it to be a place of habitation in my life.

Worshiping Him is more than just singing, its loving Him with pure and true emotions. It's seeing Him for who He is and all that He has done for you. It is knowing Him for His beauty and His passion for you. Seeing the things that He has been waiting to pour into your life.

Lift up your head and see the Heavens open up and the glory of God come down. It is by your faith that you lift your hands and praise the Lord. It is by your faith that you believe in all His promises. They are yes and Amen! It is by faith that we see the miracles, signs, and wonders because all these things follow His presence.

Our praise opens up the supernatural atmosphere, where anything is possible in Christ Jesus. Our praise opens up the gates for the King of Glory to come in!

"Open up, ancient gates! Open up, ancient doors, and let the King of glory enter. Who is the King of glory? The LORD, strong and mighty; the LORD, invincible in battle. Open up, ancient gates! Open up ancient doors, and let the King of glory enter. Who is the King of Glory? The LORD of *Heaven's* Armies - he is the King of *Glory."* ~ Psalms 24:7-10

Whatever is going on in your life or whatever has broken and hurt you in your past, I am here to tell you the Lord of Heaven's Army is standing right there and waiting on you to open up that old ancient gate and let Him come in. And when you do, be ready for a flood of the presence of His fire and glory. Heaven will come down and fill you with the presence of His everlasting love.

"I will praise the LORD at all times. I will constantly speak his *praises."* ~ Psalms 34:1

Once you have had an encounter with the Lord and he has touched your heart, it is not hard at all to speak His praises continually. I probably drove some people nuts with this at first, but it doesn't really matter what the world around you thinks anyway. He deserves all the praise; it will never be enough. In the Heavens, praise and worship never stops. We don't even know what that is like yet.

All I know is I am supposed to model myself after Jesus, and He worshipped and gave praise to the father at all times, and so can I.

Restoring The Garden

Back in 2009, at the beginning of the end of my marriage, the Lord began to speak to me about restoring the garden. Well, about a year prior, we had done some remodeling on our home. We remodeled the kitchen and added on a dining room. When we did the add on, it made an area on the side of our home a great little courtyard. I had put beautiful glass French doors going out into the area from the dining room and then an iron gate to exit to the outside. So, of course, when I heard restore the garden, I was thinking of the natural garden.

I was so excited because I loved the courtyard, and I could see how beautiful it was going to look with all the trees and flowers I had planned to put there. I told the Lord I was going to build Him a beautiful garden, and I did. I had a beautiful tree planted there, palm trees, two fruit trees, and beautiful flowers. I had an amazing iron swing and table. I could open the French doors and just enjoy the lovely garden.

But the Lord kept talking to me about restoring the garden. It was over a year before I understood what the Lord was actually saying to me. He wasn't talking about my courtyard, even though I am sure He was pleased because it was really beautiful. He was talking about the garden in my soul. The weeds that had grown up in my garden. He knew I loved the beauty of the garden and the flowers. He was referring to the healing He wanted to do in my soul. The Gardener needed to pull out some weeds, a lot of weeds actually.

This was when I got my first revelation of healing of soul wounds. The Lord showed it to me in this way. It was like he went inside and pulled out these old bad weeds by the roots so they would not grow back.

At the cross, Jesus restored us back to our original position in the garden. This is how the Lord wants His children to live on the earth.

This is where I spend most of my time with the Lord. In my dreams and my visions, it's always in a beautiful garden. Sometimes we are by water, sometimes sitting under a big tree, and sometimes even swimming in the water. There are always beautiful flowers like I have never seen. I love the garden.

"Take my yoke upon you. Let me teach you, because I am humble and gentle at heart, and you will find rest for your souls." ~ Matthew 11:29

Never Alone

The way I felt after my husband left me in 2009 was so strange. I was sad, but I was never afraid. Even when all my children moved away and I moved into a new home, I was never afraid. I just didn't like it because I wasn't using to being all by myself. I had not been by myself since I was 18 years old. I had always had a big family, and in an instant, it was all gone. The silence was horrible to me. I was so use to doing for people that I didn't know what to do with myself.

I just threw myself in the Word. It was the first thing I did every morning and the last thing I did at night. I got the Word of God in me any way I could, books, cds, dvd's, anything I could find. I focused on the Lord and put Him first in my life. I was not going to ever listen to the enemy again. I was never going to be alone again. I was never going to believe all the negative things that had been spoken over my life ever again. If I had to repeat it a million times a day I would. I knew who my

God was! I knew who was for me, and I knew who was against me!

"Don't be afraid, for I am with you. *Don't* be discouraged, for I am your God. I will strengthen you and help you. I will hold you up with my victorious right *hand."* ~ Isaiah 41:10

The Lord had to be my strength because I certainly didn't have enough to get through what I had to endure. I am so thankful that He taught me to lean on Him and Him alone. I think the Lord allows some situations so we can learn to trust and lean only on Him. I look at my situation now, at what I have come through, and I am so grateful for the strength that He gave me to endure it all.

"Teach these new disciples to obey all the commands I have given you. And be sure of this: I am with you always, even to the end of the *age."* ~ Matthew 28:20

Jesus Himself tells us here that we can be sure of this, that He is right here with us! He is always with us, and He will be with us even to the end of the age!

Our Comforter

When you believe in Jesus Christ as your Lord and Savior, the Holy Spirit comes to live and abide inside of you. As a young child at the age of 10 when I received the Lord, I never really understood the meaning of that. I knew I was saved and would go to

Heaven, but I never knew the Kingdom of Heaven came into me.

When I began to read and pray and learn about the Holy Spirit, He totally rocked my world. He is the Spirit of the living God, and He is here with me always. No matter where I go or what I do, He is here with me, living inside me. Just trying to explain what He is to me now is not easy because He is my everything.

Holy Spirit is the one I talk to all the time. When I go on my walks and people pass by, they are probably wondering who I'm talking to. That's one of my favorite times of the day. He is the one who comforts me at night, which can sometimes still be a hard time for me. He knows how to bring me joy at just the time I need it. He is my teacher, who has taught me so much about the Kingdom, with so much more to teach than I can imagine.

He is teaching me to listen and respond to His promptings. It's so exciting when you actually hear and respond correctly. At times, when I would miss the mark, I would feel so bad. But now I am not hard on myself like that anymore because I realized it was not about me getting something right or wrong, it was just about my willingness to listen and respond to the Holy Spirit.

Holy Spirit is always showing us something. He may be giving you a thought of a person. Ask Him what it is you are to do. Maybe you are just to pray for that person. He may be showing you something in your life that is keeping you from a healing, something that keeps repeating over and over. Pay close attention to these things. I had this happen to me just recently. I heard the Holy Spirit tell me I needed to be drinking water. I heard the word, and I knew I didn't drink enough, but I still did not increase my intake.

A year later, I had blood work done and a hair analysis test done. I was seriously dehydrated, which could cause injury to my kidneys. I asked for forgiveness for that one and began to drink lots more water. Holy Spirit is looking out for everything that has to do with our lives. How to take care of our bodies so we will be in good health, how to make good choices when trying to make decisions. The Lord wants to be a part of all of your life, your spiritual, emotional, and physical well-being. He will change you day by day if you just let go and let Him have His way.

Let the beauty and the glory of His tangible Spirit come and fill you with His presence. Invite Him into the deepest places of your heart and let the power of His love over take you and heal you and make you whole. Come, Holy Spirit, come!

"I am a special messenger from Christ Jesus to you Gentiles. I bring you the Good News so that I might present you as an acceptable offering to God, made holy, by the Holy Spirit." ~ Romans 15:16

Angels

"Therefore, angels are only servants — spirits sent to care for people who will inherit *salvation."* ~ Hebrew 1:14

The Bible says we are not to worship angels, but we are to believe that they are real and they are here among us. The angels of the Lord, the faithful ones, are sent here to help us, to aid us. The Bible says that the angels harken to the Word of the Lord. When we decree our words into the atmosphere, the angels harken to the Word of the Lord, and His Word never fails.

"Praise the LORD, you angels, you mighty ones who carry out his plans, listening for each of his *commands."* ~ Psalms 103:20

I know the Lord has sent His angels to watch over us and to protect us as we follow Him.

"If you make the LORD your refuge, if you make the Most High your shelter, no evil will conquer you; no plague will come near your home. For he will order his angels to protect you wherever you go. They will hold you up with their hands so you *won't* even hurt your foot on a *stone."* ~ Psalms 91:9-12

In less than two years, I had three really bad falls. One was at my son's house. I got my high heels hung up in a gate and fell backwards, pulling the gate out of the wall with me onto a tile floor. I cracked my head, my back, and my hip. I couldn't move. I felt a tingling in my body when I fell. It wasn't good. My son checked me out and drove me home, thinking I might have injured my back or hip. I kept feeling the back of my head because I couldn't believe I didn't crack it wide open. I had hit the floor just that hard. The kids heard it all the way outside.

As I was lying in bed that night, I remembered I had just gone to a healing service at Love Gospel Church to hear Joan Hunter. She told a story about how she had to minister at a conference once and she had gotten very sick. Her throat was sore, and she was concerned about being able to talk the next day. She was lying in bed praying when she heard the Lord tell her to lay her own hands on herself. She laid hands on everyone else, she could do the same for herself. So, I laid my hand on my stomach and began to pray in the spirit. My whole body began to get warm. I never got up to check anything out, I just feel asleep.

When I woke up the next day, I put my legs over the side of the bed and was able to get up with no pain in my back or hips. My abs felt like I had done a thousand sit ups, but I was healed. I know God ordered His angels to watch over me that day. I am thankful for remembering what Joan said about using my own hands and letting God use me.

If you are struggling going through any kind of battle in your life, as we all do, the angels join you in your spiritual warfare. You are never alone. They provide comfort in the mist of your suffering.

"The winds are your messengers; fames of fire are your *servants."* ~ Psalms 104:4

The angels are like flames of fire, like the breath of God, His Holy fire! And they are dispatched from Heaven by our Father on our behalf. Isn't it time that we as children of God wake up and acknowledge that we have an innumerable number of angels of God waiting to partner with us to do the works of the Kingdom here on earth. Let us join with the angels and Praise the Lord!

"Praise him, all his angels! Praise him, all the armies of *heaven!"* ~ Psalms 148:2

I am fully convinced that God ordered His angels to protect me all my life. They were there protecting me when I was alone as a child and needing help. They were there when I was in the hospital as a young married teenage girl. They took my baby home to be with the Lord. They were there with me when my heart was broken and I took too many drugs. They protected me from death. They were there protecting me once again when I was at death's door during the birth of my son. They were there watching over my other two children during birth. Angels were always surrounding me during my divorce, protecting me in that dark time. They are with me all the time when I praise and worship the Lord.

I can't even imagine the numerous amounts of angels that God has sent on my behalf over my lifetime to keep me safe. God is not done with me. He has great and awesome things for me to do to advance the Kingdom. He is not done with any of us. Isn't it amazing how we can partner with the angels, these messengers of God, to advance His Kingdom.

Chapter 9

Made in His Image

When I think of the image of My God, I think of a likeness to Him. Physically, we are all so different. Not one of us are created the same, but I believe that you can be around someone for so long that you start to look a lot like that person. Haven't you seen married couples that have been married for so many years that they seem to look a lot alike? I believe you can start to take on the form and likeness of a person that you spend lots of time with.

"So God created human beings in his own image. In the image of God he created them; male and female he created *them.*" ~ Genesis 1:27

"Christ is the visible image of the invisible God. He existed before anything was created and is supreme over all creation..." ~ Colossians 1:15

I believe the more time we spend in the presence of our Father God, the more we will take on the likeness of Him, the likeness that He created in us. The way to do this is to be in His Word. When you want more of Him, you will have a hunger and a thirst for more of His Presence. Our godlikeness is the pathway to our greatest joy and fulfillment. This is the place where we will be our best, when we are fully developed into God's image. It's not ever going to be found in a person, a place, or a thing in this world, only in God. The place of glory to glory!

"So all of us who have had that veil removed can see and reflect the glory of the LORD. And the LORD - who is the Spirit - makes us more and more like him as we are changed into his glorious *image."* ~ 2 Corinthians 3:18

We are the image of Christ. We are to be more than a witness to Him, we are to be the witness. When we approach people, they should see Jesus in us, His Glory, His Light. If they don't know Him, any darkness will be exposed in the light that we carry! Nothing and no one can hide their darkness from the Light! Just watch how people will react to your light.

Fear of the Lord

When I was growing up and going to church, I was always taught that Jesus loved me. I had no doubts that He did. But I was also taught that there was a God in the Heavens that would punish me if I did wrong. In the Baptist church that I grew up in, we were taught it wasn't right to dance, and I loved to dance. But when I went to school dances, I would always wonder if I was doing something wrong. I saw God as someone who was always watching to correct us for our wrongs rather than a loving God. I grew up with such a lack of the true knowledge of who my Father was. For it says in the Word of God that we are to fear the Lord, for to fear Him is the beginning of our understanding and our knowledge. But I had a different understanding and definition of the word fear. Fear to me was to bring complete panic to my heart. I associated it with danger and pain.

"Fear of the LORD is the foundation of true wisdom. All who obey his commandments will grow in *wisdom.*"
~ Psalms 111:10

"The Fear of the LORD is the foundation of wisdom. Knowledge of the Holy One results in good judge*ment.*"
~ Proverbs 9:10

When I read the Word of God from the beginning to the end, I began to get an idea about what the fear of the Lord really meant. It is never about being afraid of Him because everything He ever does is for the good of His people. We have to believe that what God does is always for our own good, but He will not tolerate the sins of this world. When I think of fearing the Lord, I think of honoring Him in all His glory. We cannot come against, compromise, or water down His Word. For He is an awesome, powerful, and mighty God. We must embrace the Lion as well as the Lamb.

God began to show me that the fear I had was not of Him. It was fear from the ruler of this world, satan. It was a completely different kind of fear. It was harmful, torturing, murdering, and caused death. I received so much freedom and healing, letting go of all the old beliefs that I had been holding on to. I am forever grateful for Holy Spirit and for the knowledge and the wisdom of the Lord. The foundation of His Word is my new way of living.

How great it is to live in this knowledge and wisdom. How wonderful it is to have this understanding of my Father.

Who I Was

I was a young girl who fell in love at seventeen and married the love of my life at nineteen. He was the one man I felt I could trust the minute we met. I had lost trust in men. I wasn't sure who I could trust when I was violated by my grandfather.

I was a young woman that was betrayed by the man that I loved. The pain was more than I could bare. I had given myself to him, and now he had been with another. I felt so ashamed of myself. I couldn't deal with the guilt. I wanted a way out of my pain.

I was a young woman with an unforgiving heart. I never forgave him for what he had done to me. I became bitter and angry, and I hid it well so I would not lose him. This root went deep down in my heart and grew all through the years of my life and my marriage, causing sickness, disease, and bitterness. Bitterness destroys!

As a young woman, I had to decide if I should keep my baby or terminate the pregnancy that had gone wrong.

That decision caused pain and sorrow that no woman or mother should ever have to go through at nineteen or any age.

I was a young woman who sinned against her husband with adultery because he had done the same to me. The first time, I did it out of the anger that had built up in my heart because I couldn't understand how my love for him wasn't enough and how he had so casually and easily cast my love away.

Later in life, when it happened again, it was out of pure loneliness. There were so many broken and missing pieces of my heart. I just needed to be loved and was tired of always being alone.

Renewing My Mind

"Put on your new nature, and be renewed as you learn to know your Creator and become like *him."*
~ Colossians 3;10

".... Christ is all that matters, and he lives in all of *us"*
~ Colossians 3:11

"Since God chose you to be holy people he loves, you must clothe yourselves with tenderhearted mercy, kindness, humility, gentleness, and patience. Make allowance for each *other's* faults, and forgive anyone who offends you. Remember, the LORD forgave you, so you must forgive others. Above all, clothe yourself with love, which binds us all together in perfect

harmony. And let the peace that comes from Christ rule in your hearts. For as members of one body you are called to live in peace. And always be thankful. Let the message about Christ, in all its richness, fill your lives. Teach and counsel each other with all the wisdom he gives. Sing psalms and hymns and spiritual songs to God with thankful hearts. And whatever you do or say, do it as a representative of the LORD Jesus, giving thanks through him to God the *Father."* ~ Colossians 3:12-17

As I grew to know my Abba Father, my eyes opened as to who I truly am. If I was created in Him as He says I am, I could not be all the things that I had become in this world. Since my Father is Truth and He cannot lie, if I am going to believe anyone, it is Him for sure!

"Jesus told them, *"I am the way, the truth, and the life."* ~ John 14:6

My Father chose me to be a part of His holy family. He created me for that purpose. That alone completely changed the way I thought of myself. No matter what I looked like at the time, He wanted me. All He saw in me was beauty and holiness. He trusted me and loved me enough to send His son to die for me. He wanted me at that very moment, when I was at the worst I had ever been in my life. I never knew a love and a trust like this before.

I had developed a victim's spirit. You know you have a victim mentality when you try to justify wrong and stay in a situation where you are being abused. In most cases, you stay for the children, for financial reasons, or because you love them. Victims avoid facing the truth and deceive themselves about hard situations. I had fallen into this pit and couldn't even see it because I had been there for so long. All of my friends left my side. They could not bear to watch any more. It's a horrible and sinful place to be. I had to choose to walk out the truth, even if it did not feel good. I had to make a choice to let go of feelings and embrace the truth of the Word of God and the words that He was bringing to me over this process of healing.

I made a decision in my life to choose Jesus, the Truth and the Way! The victim's spirit that had entered my life as a young girl is now gone in the Name of Jesus. It supernaturally left the instant I turned my life back to Jesus and gave it all to Him. Every demon connected to that spirit had to go, and Jesus has filled me with His glory!

I have given the Lord all the wrong thinking that I had had in my life and also all the wrong things that were spoken over me. The Lord has turned all these things around in my life. I am now doing all the things that I thought I could never do. I thought I could never live one day of my life single, but I am actually living my life fuller and healthier than I have in over thirty-eight years. I am free from the chronic pain that I suffered for over thirty-eight years. That is a miracle, and I Praise God! God has completely renewed my way of thinking about Him and His possibilities. He is the God of ALL THINGS. There is nothing He can't and won't do in my life and in your life if you let Him renew your mind into the likeness of His.

Dreams & Visions

I absolutely love dreams. I have always had lots of dreams. Even as a child, I remember having many dreams. I can still recall having dreams where I would be flying in the spirit, even though I did not know what being in the spirit meant back then. All I knew was I would wake up with the feeling that I had really been flying. Sometimes I would be in a room in someone's home or a building where people were, but I would be in the ceiling looking down at people. It was so cool and so very real. I had many of these dreams about flying.

I would also have some not so good dreams about cats as a kid. I remember being chased by a lot of cats into a dark basement. I had this dream more than once, and I could not understand why I would have the same dream over and over. But now I understand it was a dream from the enemy to bring me fear.

Once in my younger years, I had a dream that my grandfather was standing at the foot of my bed. I saw him as clear as if my eyes were open. He had passed away when I was 17. I asked him why he was there, and he said he had come to get my grandmother. I just told him he couldn't have her, and he went away. I told my mother about the dream the next day because my grandmother had been sick, and she said my grandmother had suffered a massive heart attack and her heart had stopped for over a minute, but they revived her. I will never forget that dream or vision.

We know that all through the Bible it talks about dreams and visions. God has always talked to His people through them. Through these pictures, in our imagination, He speaks to us. Sometimes they may be difficult to figure out, but with the help of the Holy Spirit, the answer will come in time. I have had a dream that I thought meant one thing, but months or years later when it played out, realized what the Lord meant. I always try to remember the dreams I have and write them down in a journal, even if they seem insignificant.

For me, those "insignificant" ones have been the ones that were a powerful message from the Lord. Sometimes I think it means one thing and I will go back to it months or a year later and the Lord will reveal a new thing. That's why it is good to journal them and ask and wait on the Lord. I find that the Lord will always speak to you as an individual, in a language that you will understand in your dream. He wants to speak to you personally, to show you how much He loves and adores you.

Walking Through The Valley

It seemed like when I began walking through this season of my life with the Lord, I became flooded with dreams. I had always been a dreamer, but I hadn't recalled remembering dreams so well and having so many different dreams in one night. They would seem like the craziest dreams sometimes, and most all of my dreams were about me and my husband. I had other dreams also, but at least seventy percent of my dreams still pertained to my life with him. I constantly questioned the Lord as to why I continued to have all these dreams. I believe God was helping me find forgiveness in issues where no forgiveness was ever given in the marriage.

I would record the dream, write down what I felt the Lord was saying to me about the dream, pray about it, and then ask for forgiveness where I needed to. Then I would let it go. This has gone on for almost 6 years.

To give you an example, this is a dream I had in February of 2014. I was being held captive by my ex-husband. He was yelling for some men to help him. There were 4 or 5 men, and they all had guns. They were all trying to hurt me and hold me down. The place was dark. I didn't recognize where I was or any of the faces. I remember calling out the Name of the Lord — and leaving down a hallway.

I asked the Lord to give me some understanding of what the dream meant. He said, "The guns were weapons, words, and accusations. The other gunmen represented the accuser of the brethren." This was a dream showing me how to pray about the abusive words that had been spoken to me, words that had hurt me during my marriage. I was able to forgive, rebuke the enemy, and give it to God.

There is nothing God won't do, and I am so amazed how He uses our dreams to heal our wounds. God will take us through whatever process we need to build our faith and trust in Him.

Future Plans

I realized that in a lot of my dreams, the Lord was giving me all these wonderful new plans, plans that I believe have been there all along. The reason I say that is because I dream things that I sometimes recall dreaming when I was a child. So, that leads me to believe that He is restoring all things back to what they should have been.

In February of 2014, I had another dream. I was in a line at a food market. There was a lady putting lots of food on the belt. The belt was going straight up. When she got all of her food on the belt, she went up also. Then a man that was standing in front of me was putting his food on the belt. I could only see this man from the back. He was leaving some of his things. As I was trying to help him put his things on the belt before he went up, this huge head of lettuce fell down from the lady's food. I picked it up and gave it to her and told her it had fallen from her things. (I noticed the food was huge) I began to put my food on the belt. I remember asking, "Why was it so far to reach?" I was having to stretch really far to reach the belt. I had to throw some of my things to get them up there!

I saw this as a good dream. I was feeding on the Word of God and ascending up to a higher place. God was really stretching me for what He was preparing for me. I was going up with others too, meaning I was ascending into the Heavens and helping others along the way.

I also had another dream in the month of February of that same year. It was very rare that I would ever have a dream that was not good, but we know the enemy still comes in to steal and rob us and try to mess up God's plans. In this dream, I was hanging on a ledge, like on top of a wall. I saw demons. I could actually see their awful faces trying to pull me off the ledge. I had never had a dream like this before. They were pulling on my leg and grabbing at my arm. I remember just watching them and staring at them. Their efforts were of no use. They could not move me. Finally, I called out the name of Jesus, and I saw them no more!

I asked the Lord about this dream because I don't usually have dreams like that. He said the enemy is trying to pull you down from where I (the Lord) am taking you.

I always keep my eyes on Jesus and no one else. When God is for us, who can ever be against us.

In March of 2014, I had a dream I was in Heaven and Jesus and I was swinging on a swing set, just like the ones we had on our school playgrounds when I was growing up. I always loved to swing. Jesus asked me how high did I want to go. I said, "As high as we possibly can!" So, we kept getting higher and higher until, finally, I realized I had better grab hold of His hand. As soon as I took hold of His hand, we went from swinging to soaring!

It was crazy fun! This has been just one of my many flying dreams with Jesus.

There are so many ways the Lord will come and speak to you in your dreams and visions. He loves you and wants to meet with you on this intimate level. He will show you things that only you will relate to because He knows everything about you. Let the Lord open up this world of dreaming with Him to you.

Passionately In Love

One weekend, I attended a conference for the Seer Anointing at XP Ministries with Patricia King. It was such an amazing day with the tangible presence of the Lord. During our break, I felt like I just wanted to go spend some time alone in the presence of the Lord, so I went and sat in my car and ate a little and then prayed in the spirit. As I prayed, I had a vision of the color purple. It was like everything was turning this beautiful shade of purple. As I continued to pray and press in, the purple color began to turn into purple roses. They were on the ground, on vines, everywhere. It was amazing! I could even smell the fragrance of the roses. It was the most beautiful vision I had ever seen because roses are my absolute favorite flower. I could smell the fragrance of roses all day long.

As I was looking at all of the beautiful roses, I suddenly saw Jesus holding a bouquet of the roses in His hand, and He hands them to me. A feeling of love came over me that was so unexplainable. I took the roses from Him, took one out of the bouquet, and gave it back to Him. The power of love was unexplainable. That was all I remember of the vision. When I woke out of the vision, I was in tears in my car, but I was filled with a love that I had never felt before.

I asked the Lord why the roses were purple. I knew the Lord had chosen roses because He knew that was my favorite flower, but I have always bought the red rose. I knew purple meant royalty, and I knew that I was His beloved and royalty in His eyes, but there was something more He wanted me to know about the vision.

The Lord said, "I have been passionately in love with you before you were ever born." The Lord was telling me how much He loved me, and I could actually feel the presence of that passionate love in the vision. I looked up the lavender rose and found that it is a sign of enchantment and love at first sight. Those who have been enraptured by feelings of love and adoration have used lavender roses to express their romantic feelings and intentions.

I have been raptured by His love! My Father adores me, this I know. This encounter with the Lord has given me an assurance of His love for me that no words could ever explain. It was a tangible presence of His passion that came upon me that no one can ever take away.

He has this same love and passion for you. God is endless. There is absolutely no end to His love!

Hunger

When you get a taste of His love and passion, all you want is more. We will spend all eternity loving Him and knowing Him. There is just no end to Him. My heart's desire is to know Him more, but not in a religious way. I am free to love Him because He loves me first. I am free to worship Him in so many ways. I stay close to Him by praying to Him and hearing His voice and staying in His Word. Staying in the Word is so important. God's Word is truth, and I want His truth to be rooted deep down within me.

"Jesus replied, *"*I am the bread of life. Whoever comes to me will never be hungry again. Whoever believes in me will never be *thirsty"* ~ John 6:35

When we come to Him and let Him fill us up with His love, knowledge, and wisdom, we will lack nothing to be able to live our lives as we should. Our hunger to abide in Him daily and desire to do His will as He asks will lead us into our destiny in Him.

Love Never Ends

His love for me and you will never end. There is nothing in Heaven or earth that can ever take it away. It is an endless supply and overflow of love. Everyone is looking for this perfect love! Everyone has a need for love, and it's His deep, profound, true, sincere, love that they are searching for.

"The faithful love of the LORD never ends! His mercies never *cease"* ~ Lamentations 3:22

"I pray that from his glorious, unlimited resources he will empower you with inner strength through his *Spirit."* ~ Ephesians 3:16

God promises His unlimited resource of love to you and me. He WILL empower us with inner strength through the Holy Spirit. The strength of His love will give power to any of your weaknesses. His love is healing to any sickness that may be in your body, whether it be emotional or physical. His love will bring joy to the brokenhearted. He is the perfect love that is the only ointment to heal. The power of His love brought life to our dying souls.

"But those who trust in the LORD will find new strength. They will soar high on wings like eagles. They will run and not grow weary. They will walk and not *faint."* ~ Isaiah 40:31

"Let all that I am praise the LORD; may I never forget the good things he does for me. He forgives all my sins and heals all my *diseases."* ~ Psalms 103:2-3

"He heals the brokenhearted and bandages their *wounds."* ~ Psalms 147:3

"He redeems me from death and crowns me with love and tender *mercies."* ~ Psalms 103:4

In the Garden

This is the place where I have been for years. I see myself walking with Jesus in the garden and talking about the things that were going on in my life. Sometimes we would be sitting underneath this huge tree, just sitting and talking. Other times we would be sitting on a blanket by the river having a picnic. I remember holding the Lord's hand and walking through fields of flowers in a beautiful sundress. The flowers were so tall. Everything is so beautiful and peaceful in this place. It's quiet and calm, and the smell is amazing. There are flowers, trees, and plants everywhere, and the colors are beautiful. Sometimes I am just there with the Lord, just being with Him in His presence because that is where I wanted to be, I needed His love. I needed His healing. I felt safe there. I felt comfortable there. I didn't want to leave. I stayed in this place for 5 years while the Lord was healing me from all my trauma.

Then I had a word from the Lord that it was time to come out of the garden. I had built a wall around myself in the garden because I knew I was safe there. When I heard that word, I knew it was right. I had found my safe place and did not want to leave it and get hurt again. But the Lord had so much that He wanted me to do, and He couldn't fulfill His purpose in me if I stayed hidden in the garden. He assured me that I could come in and out of the garden anytime I wanted, I just didn't need to stay there anymore.

"My lover has gone down to his garden, to his spice beds, to browse in the gardens and gather the lilies. I am my *lover's,* and my lover is mine. He browses among the *lilies."* ~ Song of Songs 6:2-3

Chapter 10

Miracles & Healings

As I look back over my life, it is so obvious to me that the presence of the Lord has been with me all the time. Over these past few years, I have had time to spend in the quietness with Him and remember so many things. When I needed Him most, He was always there. If He had not been, I would not be here today. There were so many times in my life when I cried out to Him for help, and He was always there even when I never deserved it. I was not living as a child of God, but He was always there for me no matter what I was doing. I know this to be true about my Father God, He will never abandon me. One of the most important things in my life is knowing that I will never be abandoned again. My Father has made this promise to me, and this promise is also for you. So, we never have to be afraid or discouraged ever again.

He is with us now, and He will be with us through all eternity.

"Do not be afraid or discouraged, for the LORD will personally go ahead of you. He will be with you; he will neither *fail you nor abandon you.*" ~ Deuteronomy 31:8

Freedom From Chronic Pain

I had lived for thirty-eight years with two to four migraines a month and even suffered mild strokes. It was a complete nightmare! The wounds in my soul from my childhood had brought on this physical condition. The trauma of the abortion was also a major cause. The migraines started soon after. The cause of my migraines was rooted in guilt. I never got over the guilt of not knowing if I had made a good decision, thinking later in life, it was never my decision to make. This guilt came from a conflict I was having within myself and because I internalized my feelings, it produced even more guilt. There was low self-esteem, shame, and self-hatred. This was who I was for all those years until Christ Jesus set me free!

I even had anger toward my husband at the time because he never talked about losing our child. I wanted to talk about it. I wanted to know if he ever thought about it as much as I did. Every time Holy Spirit would bring up the subject, I would receive more forgiveness in this area. It was a long, long process, but I began to get a deeper understanding of forgiving from my heart and not just from my head.

One day I was praying and asking the Lord how He could ever be happy with me for letting go of my child? This is what I heard Him say, "My dear child, if I were mad at you, would I have given you three more beautiful perfectly healthy children?" I was undone. I knew He was not mad at me but had deep love and mercy for me. I forgave myself. I forgave the way I had been thinking about my husband and his feelings.

During my divorce trial in 2011, I suffered a severe migraine and two mild strokes. That has been the last migraine I have had since the Lord Jesus Christ has set me free!

If there is anyone reading this book that is suffering with chronic pain, I am here to tell you there is hope! I was told by doctors I would never be healed. I went without hope for thirty-eight years. Even though I was a Christian who had been brought up in church and went to church off and on during my adult life, no one ever told me that Jesus was the same today as yesterday. Our hope is Jesus the healer. He is everything you need to be healed and whole in your body, spirit, and soul.

Freedom From Spirit of Suicide

When I took an overdose of drugs at the age of eighteen, I was at a point of weakness. I was experiencing an emotional shock at the moment, and in my weakness, all the walls of my defenses were down. It left me vulnerable for the enemy to attach himself. It wasn't hard when it came to the drugs because they lower our defenses, and demons thrive on weakness. They love to move right in. When I committed this sin, it gave the enemy a legal right to affect me and bother me in all kinds of ways. I had opened a door to the enemy in my life. Off and on in my life I would have issues of depression. I had a serious time with it after what I went through with my last pregnancy, but I never got help. Later in life, I saw doctors and was given medication, but I would always stop taking the medicine. I never liked the way it made me feel. I had many suicidal thoughts, especially the last fifteen years or so with the migraines, marital issues, and the divorce.

Suicidal thoughts are nothing to play around with or to make light of. This spirit of suicide has a strong force and a strong pull. There is only one way out of this darkness, and that is Jesus. He is the Light that will take away all the darkness!

It was in the forgiveness of the bitterness that I was holding in my heart that I was set free! My boyfriend had caused a traumatic experience for me all those years ago, and I was holding it against him. I had to forgive him for hurting me and repent for holding on to the bitterness in my heart. I also asked for forgiveness for myself and repented for taking the drugs. Now I am Free! Christ has set me free! Everyday that I wake up, I am happy and glad to be alive. I thank God every morning for every day I have. I tell Him every morning what a beautiful day it is!

"But if we confess our sins to him, he is faithful and just to forgive us our sins and to cleanse us from all *wickedness."* ~ 1John 1:9

I had a vision once where the Lord was taking all the pain, hurt, and bitterness out of my heart. Then he opened His hand and was holding a beautiful, heart-shaped, pink diamond, and He replaced my heart with it, changing a heart of bitterness to a heart of His love.

They say pink diamonds are very rare and one of the most popular of the gemstones. They symbolize love, romance, creativity, and femininity,

Freedom From Fear of Man

For as long as I can remember I have had the fear of what others thought about me. So much so that it kept me from doing so many things in life. This may come to you as a surprise, but none of us are immune from this issue known as the fear of man. It's the power of the world, our flesh, and the enemy has over us. Always telling us what we need to have, what we need to wear, that we need more of this and more of that. Did I say the right thing? Did I do the right thing? So worried about pleasing people that we lose focus on what truly matters.

It is only by the grace of Jesus Christ, - who is grace Himself, do we overcome the fear of man. A work of grace is something God does in us and through us when we submit ourselves to Him. We can't buy it, nor can we earn it. It is a gift from God.

"For the grace of God has been revealed, bringing salvation to all people. And we are instructed to turn from godless living and sinful pleasures. We should live in this evil world with wisdom, righteousness, and

devotion to God, while we look forward with hope to that wonderful day when the glory of our great God and Savior, Jesus Christ, will be revealed . He gave his life to free us from every kind of sin, to cleanse us, and to make us his very own people, totally committed to *doing good deeds."* ~ Titus 2:11-14

The better we know the Word of God, the more intimate we will know the God of the Word. And the more intimate we are with God, the stronger His presence is in our lives. There is nothing like the presence of God. When we live in His presence, in His Glory, we will no longer be afraid of what other people think of us! It was like a supernatural healing. It just came with having a personal relationship with the Lord, spending time with Him, receiving His love and loving Him, letting His love fill me to the point that nothing around me comes before Him.

"Jesus responded, " Didn't I tell you that you would see God's glory if you believe?" ~ John 11:40

I am not a slave to this world. My chains have been broken. I am free! Whom the Son of Man sets free is truly free!

"For I am not ashamed of this Good News about Christ. It is the power of God at work, saving everyone who believes - the Jew *first and also the Gentile."* ~ Romans 1:16

Transition

When my ex and I separated, I found myself in a whole new world of transitions! I didn't know where to start or how to manage the worldly things outside of my household responsibilities. I didn't know how to be me when the other half of me was torn. I didn't know how to be a family when the family was torn apart.

I was having to leave our home of over 20 years. I had no idea where I was going to go. I had never made a move alone before. I had never bought a home. I had never even bought a car before. My husband did those things. But there was no one around anymore. All the kids had moved out. I think the Lord wanted it this way. He wanted no one there but Him for me to depend on. It was one of the hardest times I have ever gone through, but I pressed into Him, trusted Him, and I made it through the transition. I believe the hardest times are the times God will show up the greatest and the strongest in our lives. He did for me, and He will for you. Our God is always with us, and He will always make a way for us in our hard times. He has walked with me through every valley, and gone before me and removed mountains. He is teaching me to trust Him in all things and how to overcome the things of this world.

There are still mountains ahead of me to come down, but I look at them now, and I just want to laugh. For my eyes have seen the miracles of the mountains He has already removed. For the Lord says to trust Him, for He will give you bread for today and not to worry about tomorrow. So, I don't worry about those mountains because I know they are coming down too.

"This is my command - be strong and courageous! Do not be afraid or discouraged. For the LORD your God is with you *wherever you go."* ~ Joshua 1:9

When I was trying to start packing to move out of the family home, I would freeze up. I would come home and sit in the car in my garage and just look at all the stuff and say, "Oh Lord, where in the world do I even start?" I would think of the closets that were so full of things that had been there for so many years. I would then think of the attic space. I had never even been up there in all the years we lived in the home. I was just completely overwhelmed, so I would do nothing.

I just continued to pray, and one day, I had peace about it. I felt ready to start cleaning things out. Little by little, I started going through things, letting things go, and packing things up. There were many days when I would be too emotional to continue. One day as I was going through some of our family things, I began to weep and when I finally stopped, I noticed there were these beautiful white feathers around me. I had been surrounded and comforted by the angels of the Lord. I felt the Lord was helping me get through this difficult time.

There was another time I was sitting in my chair. I looked up, and a beautiful feather just appeared out of the air. I opened my hand to catch it. This one was quite large. I saw the angel feathers all through my process of moving and going through the transition of leaving the old home that I had loved. One morning I was in my bathroom getting dressed and praising the Lord, I felt like someone touched me and brushed around me. I turned around suddenly. I knew it was an angel.

The Lord God had sent His mighty angels, just like He promises in His Word to give me all the help I needed to move. I needed so much emotional help during this time. There is nothing that our God will not do for me and you to get us through the transitions of life. He will call forth legions and legions of His mighty angels to get you there.

"For he will order his angels to protect you where ever *you go."* ~ Psalms 91:11

A New Home

When I started looking for a new home, it was almost funny because in the natural, I had no means of getting a home. During my divorce, I had been connected to the most wonderful group of women in the business world who knew the Lord and had helped me get my life back in order. I believe all of these were divine appointments. God knows exactly who you need in your life and when and where you will need them, but they were all telling me and advising me that there was no possible way I could purchase a home. There were still unresolved issues from the divorce. Plus, there were no finances for a down payment.

I just kept believing and praying about it because as much as I never wanted to leave my old home, I felt it was the Lord telling me I needed to go. It was time for me to move, but I didn't know how it was going to happen.

Then I started receiving letters in the mail stating that I had a sum of money in an account that my ex and I use to have with his company. I thought it was just old information that was still coming in from the divorce. A month later, I got another letter with a different amount. So I thought, "Why am I still seeing this?" I called my girlfriend who was taking care of my affairs. She checked into it and found that I indeed had money in the account. This was my first financial miracle. This was my on-time miracle for my down payment. God always shows up at the right time. However, in the natural, I still couldn't buy a home because of everything that had been left in my name after the divorce. Well, I kept looking at homes anyway. I kept my focus on what I was hearing from the Lord, that I was supposed to leave my old home.

I found an area that I loved. I was looking for a small one level home, but my friend told me that area rarely had any available. A couple of weeks later, I saw this beautiful home with hardwood floors in a dream. I even saw the beautiful counter tops and framed mirrors in the bathrooms. It was such a cool dream! The next morning, as I was looking at some homes that my friend had emailed to me, I saw this house that looked just like the house in my dream. When I realized that it was in the area that I loved, I called my realtor friend and said, "I found my house. God showed it to me in a dream. Then you sent it to me in an email." When she looked it up, she found that six offers had been made on the house. She said I needed to offer up. I told her I couldn't but to tell the seller that I would give her what she was asking, even though I had not even seen the house in the natural.

She called the lady and told her who I was and a little about me. The next morning, the seller called and sold me her home! God's plans were greater than any bank's plans! Trust in the Lord your God and what He says and the plans He has for you, not what others say you can and can't do. He is far above everything and anything that we can imagine!

"And we are confident that he hears us whenever we ask for anything that pleases him." ~ 1John 5:14

"And this same God who takes care of me will supply all your needs from his glorious riches, which have been given to us in Christ Jesus. Now all glory to God our Father forever and ever! Amen." ~ Philippians 4:19 -20

Financial Miracles

"The LORD was with Joseph, so he succeeded in everything he did as he served in the home of his Egyptian master. Potiphar noticed this and realized that the LORD was with Joseph, giving him success in everything he did." ~ Genesis 39:2-3

I love the story of Joseph because whether he was in prison or the palace, he always succeeded. It's because the Lord was always with Joseph. He never took his eyes off the Lord. This is for every one of us today, all God's children who seek Him, the fullness of His Glory, and His presence. It is the power and the presence of the Lord God in us that will bring forth the things of Heaven into the earth. Everything that we need to live in His will for His Kingdom will be given to us because the Lord our God is with us. It is by Him and through Him that we are successful in life. When we have a need, He has already met that need. There is nothing too great for our God.

The Lord my God is with me just like He was with Joseph, and I will succeed in everything I do when I am in His will, and so can you!

"Remember the LORD your God. He is the one who gives you power to be successful, in order to fulfill the *covenant he confirmed to your ancestors with an oath."*
~ Deuteronomy 8:18

During my divorce proceedings, I had an attorney that did not have my best interest at heart, especially not the emotional side of it all. I guess they have to be insensitive to your feelings. I was so caught up in the fog of the emotional trauma that I never paid attention to all of the criminal events that were taking place between my lawyer and my ex-husband's lawyer. They knew each other very well and had worked together before. Once my lawyer took all the finances from me that he could, he abandoned me before the divorce was final. Knowing nothing that had gone on during the trial, I had to find a new lawyer to come in and take over the case.

During all that time, the lawyer kept billing me for more money. He accepted me as a client, knowing that I was a homemaker with no income outside of my husband's. He had told me that that was not a problem and that he had never lost a case and was not worried about getting paid. For almost three years, the bills totaling 89,109.88 never stopped coming in. Finally, in January of 2013, I received notice that he was suing me for this amount. I felt I was really being used and taken advantage of again. I talked to my lawyer, who was a good friend, and he went over everything that had happened with the case and found that my ex-lawyer had been unethical. He suggested we countersue him.

It was a major process. My girlfriend, the wife of my lawyer, and I had to go through all the divorce papers and recopy them and send them back to him. When we did, we prayed over them, we anointed them, and we took this case to the courts of Heaven and asked the Lord for His divine justice. I asked the Lord for forgiveness for anything I might have said or done wrong during the trial. I forgave my lawyer for the things he had done on my behalf. I gave the whole process to the Lord. We boxed it up and sent it off.

I received a letter in the mail on January 7, 2013 from the judge that stated, "Court ordered no action."

God is a miracle working God!

God will show justice to the just. He will protect those who do right. No matter how big your mountain is, God is bigger. No matter what others do to you, live with honesty and integrity in your heart. Your character is so important. Know how big your God is, and all these other things become possible.

"No, you have come to Mount Zion, to the city of the living God, the heavenly Jerusalem, and to countless thousands of angels in a joyful gathering. You have come to the assembl*y of God's firstborn children,* whose names are written in heaven. You have come to God himself, who is the judge over all things. You have come to the spirits of the righteous ones in heaven who have now been made perfect. You have come to Jesus, the one who mediates the new covenant between God and people, and to the sprinkled blood, which speaks forgiveness instead of crying out for vengeance like the bloo*d of Abel."* ~ Hebrew 12: 22-24

"For God is the one who provides seed for the farmer and then bread to eat. In the same way, he will provide and increase your resources and then produce a great harvest of generosity *in you."* ~ 2 Corinthians 9:10

I had been in a spiritual, emotional, and physical battle when it came to finances. I had been trying to swim out of the depth of debt since my divorce, but I couldn't seem to find air. I had sold everything that was of significant value, but I was still living paycheck to paycheck. In the mist of my storm, I never stopped giving to the Lord, but there were times when I would feel like, "Oh my gosh, I really need to be paying a bill."

I know some of you out there know what I am talking about. I was so frustrated with the debt, and I felt bad about giving. I knew this was not what God had promised me. When I came back to the Lord in 2009, the first scripture He showed me was Matthew 6:33. This became my favorite word from Him.

"Seek the Kingdom of God above all else, and live righteously, and he will give you everything you need."

He says to seek Him first in our lives, and He will give us all that we need when we live according to His ways. I have been seeking His glory and His presence since that day.

The Lord began to speak to me more about the attitude of giving. He showed me He didn't need anything extra from me. I had given Him my heart; He had given me His Son. Anything more I wanted to do would come from the love that was in me. I started seeing things from a perspective of what I had and from what God had already done in my life and not so much what I was needing or lacking.

From that day, I felt something lift off of me, like a chain that had been broken. Never again will I have that spirit come upon me. I am free to give! For freely I have received, and freely I can give! For we can never out give our God!

About a year ago, I went through an eight-month period where every month I had an unexplainable increase in my bank account. I would balance my check book myself, then rebalance it on the computer, and every month it increased by 100's. During this time, my pastor, Patricia King of XP Shiloh, was teaching that God was going to bring increase, and some of us would see increase in our accounts. Once again, I believe God was teaching me to trust Him and Him alone for everything I needed in life. If this can happen to me, it can certainly happen to you!

Father in the Name of Jesus, we thank you for who you are. We thank you that you are Jehovah Jireh, our Provider. Amen

"And this same God who takes care of me will supply all your needs from his glorious riches, which have been given to us in C*hrist Jesus."* ~ Philippians 4:19

Giving To God

"Give all your worries and cares to God, for he cares *about you."* ~ 1 Peter 5:7

I love the Word of God in this scripture. He is not telling us to give Him what we feel like giving Him and then hang on to the rest. He is telling us to give Him everything that worries us. There have been so many times when I would give something to the Lord, but if I didn't see results, I wanted to take it back. When I wasn't worrying about my own problems, I was worrying about someone else's. I had no boundaries, and I truly thought I was helping others by trying to fix their problems. Boundaries are a big thing for me. God,

I thank you that you are teaching me to have healthy boundaries!

I am so grateful and thankful for my God who cares so much about me that He asks me every day to give Him everything and anything that worries me. There is nothing too great for Him. He knows what we can and can't handle. Sometimes He will come along side of us and walk with us as we walk things out, but sometimes, we are not to battle at all. We are to rest in Him, and He will battle for us. I have found this resting place in Him. I pray you find it too.

"So there is a special rest still waiting for the people of God. For all who have entered into God's rest have rested from their labors, just as God did after creating the world." ~ Hebrew 4:9-10

During my separation from my husband and all the way through the divorce trial, I tried to hang on to our marriage. He had already left with someone else, and all I could do was send him scriptures as to what he was doing wrong in the eyes of God. No matter how angry it made him, I kept sending them. His response was negative, and I just continued to be hurt. I even did the same to my kids. I was pushing God on everyone to try and save my family. I was losing my family. I didn't know how else to fight for them. We were all falling apart, and there was so much pain. I knew God was the only healer, but I was still banging them all over the head with the Bible.

One evening at home it was just me and the Lord, spending time together. I was praying and worshiping, something I love to do. I began to see myself in the Heavens, and I was standing in front of a giant double door, when the Lord spoke to me. He said, "Sheila, I want you to pack your bags and get out of my way. I can't help your family if you don't move out of my way." I began to weep and pack my bag that happened to be right there next to me. I got all of my stuff packed and said, "Ok Lord" and left. I have not gotten in His way since then, and if I do, I will immediately repent and get out of the way.

Trying to force others to be what we want them to be is not of our Father. When you get to know who your Father is, you will know that is not His character or His heart. Our Heavenly Father does not force His love or His ways on anyone. He freely gave His Son to us, and that was my Father freely giving Himself because the Father and the Son are one. I was so sorry for ever trying to force something so Holy and so Beautiful on anyone, especially my husband and my children, the ones I loved so dearly. I have a greater understanding of it all now. My Father is so good, and everything is in His own timing. Just like it was for me.

I hope everyone who reads this will get an understanding of the love of our Father. Everything about our Father is freedom. He freely gave us His Son Christ Jesus. Jesus freely went to the cross for our sins, and Holy Spirit was freely given to us to live and dwell in us. We have the choice to freely receive Him.

Ministry

I never thought of myself being in ministry. I grew up thinking you had to be a pastor of a church to minister. I had such a wrong mindset of what ministry was. All Jesus wanted me to do was to follow Him, learn from Him, and let Him give me the gift of sharing His love with others.

"One day as Jesus was walking along the shore of the Sea of Galilee, he saw Simon and his brother Andrew throwing a net into the water, for they fished for a living. Jesus called out to them, "Come, follow me, and I will show you how to fish for people!" And they left their *nets at once and followed him."* ~ Mark 1:16-18

I believe everyone is created and able to minister the love of God. Jesus is calling each and every one of us to come and follow Him. When we learn how He loves others, how He did nothing without first hearing from the Father, how He healed the sick and the brokenhearted, we will minister in the same ways He did. We want to be just as He was here on earth, imitating His character, so people will know the passionate love the Father has for them.

The more time you spend in His presence, the more you begin to have a heart for what He has a heart for. You begin to see things through His eyes. Suddenly, things that use to matter so much to you don't seem to be so important any more.

I have such a new respect and perspective of the walk the disciples had with Jesus those three years He was here on earth. They had to have that intimate time with Him to become like Him, to be filled with His love to be able to minister to others. It's the same with us today. We have to spend years renewing our hearts and minds to become more like Him. It's a continuous journey, and we must love and embrace every moment of it.

"Imitate God, therefore, in everything you do, because you are his dear children. Live a life filled with love, following the example of Christ. He loved us and offered himself as a sacrifice for us, a pleasing aroma *to God." ~* Ephesians 5:1-2

Healing Rooms

"He comforts us in all our troubles so that we can comfort others. When they are troubled, we will be able to give them the *same comfort God has given us." ~* 2 Corinthians 1:4

It was in the mist of all my troubles that God began to use me the most. It's absolutely amazing what He did in my life. I am so thankful for the ones He put in my life during that critical time of healing. God used me to heal others as He was healing me.

As I was continuing to go through my own personal healing, I started training to minister in the Healing Rooms. When I started ministering to others, I noticed that I was receiving more and more healing of my own. As I was getting healed in areas of my life, then praying for others, I was getting blessed right back.

The Healing Rooms are a wonderful place where people can freely come to get prayer and hear from God for any need they may have. It's a place where people give of their time and love helping others come to know the power and the love of God.

It was in the Healing Rooms that I learned about praying and how to listen and hear the voice of God. It was truly like the scriptures says, I was being born again. I never knew you could pray and talk and hear the Lord like I did. My whole life was completely changed. I am so grateful that the Lord led me on this path. At the perfect time in my life, God brought me this dynamic ministry that catapulted me in my healing process. When we pray and ask God for help, He brings us the ultimate best!

If you are in a place of sorrow and pain, I assure you God has an ultimate plan for you also. Your Father dearly loves you, and He wants nothing more than for you to be set free!

XP Ministries

It was in October of 2013 that the Healing Rooms connected with XP Ministries to be a part of a Big Tent event in Phoenix. The Healing Rooms were to have a tent there to pray for people during the breaks after the speakers were done. This was a ten-day event. It was so amazing! I had never seen so many people coming for prayer. There were so many healings and deliverances. I remember after it was over, I felt the Lord was stirring something up inside of me. I prayed about it for two months, and I felt the Lord wanted me to make a move to XP Ministries.

So, in January 2014, I drove out on the first Wednesday of intercession and joined the team. I had a couple of friends that were going to come with me, but their plans changed, and they couldn't make it. I started to question if I should make the drive alone after the second week. The head intercessor that week stopped me as I was getting in my car and said she had a word from the Lord for me. It was, "Don't Retreat!" How good and on time is God? I put that on my refrigerator, and I continued to go. I did not retreat, and I have now been a part of XP Ministries for two and a half years. I can't even begin to tell you all the things that I have learned from this ministry. I have been blessed beyond words. Sometimes I just have to pray and say, "Lord, if my mind didn't get it all, I know that my Spirit man did."

I found a place that speaks the true Gospel of Jesus Christ, and it has changed my life. It complimented what I was doing in my walk, seeking the Lord first, and added so much more. It took me to even higher levels than I had been before. I was hungry and only seeking for more.

My eyes have been opened to the amazing love of my Abba Father. Everything about me has been given to me by Him. I am created exactly in His image. I see myself this way now, and not how anyone else sees me. I know that where I am in my life is exactly where He wants me and where He is going to use me to advance the Kingdom of God.

I use to feel unworthy because I was a stay home mom, but God has shown me my importance for the Kingdom and the importance of the family. It was God who created us for the purpose of having a family. He is very passionate about restoring families. It is my heart to see families restored back to the Father, their first love, and then back to each other. I am very passionate about the family mountain, because it only takes one to partner with God to restore a family.

Patricia started a ministry called WIMN. I signed up and joined the ministry group. This looks like it's going to be an exciting group of women of all walks of ministry and gifts. I am so blessed to be a part of this group of women in ministry, and I am thankful to be a part of the intercession for the ministry. I thank you, Father, for the open doors of blessing and favor!

I expect great things in my life! Be expecting great things in your life too! There is nothing your Father won't do for you! His love for you is Amazing!

"And say to Archippus," Be sure to carry out the ministry the LORD *gave you."* ~ Colossians 4:17

Chapter II

Putting My Trust in God

I can hardly put into words how I feel today compared to how I felt just seven years ago. It's like waves and waves of healing and refreshing have come over me and washed away all the ugliness. It's left me so free. I have opened the gate that was sealed shut, and all the trapped and hidden things have flown away. This was not an easy path by any means, but God doesn't promise us an easy path in this world. He just promises He is always with us as we walk through the valleys.

The door is left wide open, left wide open for the King of Kings and all His Glory to come inside and have His way. This is the best place to be in our lives, free of all hidden secrets, because when the enemy comes to prowl, we will have nothing in common with him. This is who our Jesus is, the One who inspires us to live our lives according to His example. Oh, to live in such complete love and peace!

"I don't have much more time to talk to you, because the ruler of this world approaches. He has no power over *me."* ~ John 14:30

Do you understand and know that the Spirit of the Lord lives in you and as He is, so are you? So, when the enemy approaches you, you can say the same thing, you have no power over me!

God has given us all this ability to live a life of freedom, but it is only found in receiving His Son Christ Jesus. If you have not received Him, you are not free. You are a slave to the ruler and the sins of this world. Whether you realize it or not, we were all born into this bondage, and you will stay bound up in your sickness, disease, and sorrows until you turn from them and receive Christ. This is a season when God is raising up an army of bold warriors, an army of those who Fear the Lord and will not compromise. You can't be afraid to talk about the traumas, the pain, and the issues that have tormented your life. Get them out in the open where they are not hidden anymore, and let God in all His power and glory heal you. Jesus is coming for His victorious bride, she is strong and mighty, and she is healed spirit, soul, and body.

Father, I pray that those reading this will be free from all shame and will not be afraid to expose the enemy and all his lies! I pray for each and every one who is reading this. I pray that they will be touched by the presence of Your power and Your glory. Lord Jesus, touch their hearts and fill them with the power of Your Holy Spirit. Break every chain that binds them in this world and release the freedom that comes from knowing and loving You. In Jesus Holy Name, Amen.

Childlike Faith

"At that time Jesus prayed: "O Father, LORD of heaven and earth, thank you for hiding these things from those who think themselves wise and clever, and for revealing them to the childlike." ~ Matthew 11:25

Only God holds all the answers we are looking for. When we come to Him in our humble, childlike faith, and we truly open our hearts to receive the truth of His Word, He will fill us. I spent my entire life looking for the missing piece when I had Him the whole time. I found my way to Him as a child and turned my eyes from Him as a teen. Our Father God never turns away from us. We are always the ones who turn from Him. As a teen, I suddenly became wiser and more clever and arrogant in my own knowledge as to what was best for my life. I wandered around in the wilderness for forty years because of the choices I had made, choices that separated me from God.

I am so grateful for God's mercy and grace that brought me out of the wilderness and into the promise land. He gave us this promise land so many years ago, but so many of us still moan and complain and can't seem to get out of the wilderness and cross over. I was one of those people. I didn't think I was at the time, but as I look back, I now see I seriously was. Once you seek His face and receive His grace and love, you will be able to see the promise land He has given you. Christ Jesus is the Promise. I put all my faith in Him and Him alone.

"Faith is the confidence that what we hope for will actually happen; it gives us assurance about things we cannot *see."* ~ Hebrew 11:1

I have no doubt in my heart that everything my Father reveals is truth. I know the promises that He has given me are true. He has worked miracle upon miracle upon miracle, and it has been in His timing, building my strength and character along the way. I live in the freedom of knowing my Father God, my Abba Father has everything in my life under control.

"One day some parents brought their children to Jesus so he could touch and bless them. But the disciples scolded the parents for bothering him. When Jesus saw what was happening, he was angry with his disciples. He said to them, *"Let* the children come to me. *Don't* stop them! For the Kingdom of God belongs to those who are like these children. I tell you the truth, anyone who doesn't receive the Kingdom of God like a child will never enter *it"* ~ Mark 10:13-15

So just like a child, we don't need to know all the mysteries of the Kingdom to come to Christ. Just knowing the ultimate love He gave to us on the cross should render enough. But we must come to Him, this Holy Sovereign God, with all abandonment and a need for Him in our hearts.

A couple of years ago, I had a dream. I was in the heavens with Jesus. Jesus was sitting on a little red tricycle, just like the one I had when I was a little girl. He told me to hop on the back. So, I stood on the back and held Him around His waist as He started pedaling around. We were going everywhere, laughing, and having so much fun, just like a couple of little kids. That was the most awesome dream! I remember when I woke up, I just laughed and said, "Lord, that was hilariously fun!" Now who would ever think they could have a dream like that about Jesus.

Our God is fun! He is a good, good Father. He wants us to come to Him and enjoy Him, to have this wonderful relationship with Him.

He Is My Comforter

"And I will ask the Father, and he will give you another Advocate, who will never leave *you."* ~ John 14:16

I grew up never knowing or understanding Holy Spirit as His own person, the Holy one who is here with me all the time to teach me all things about my Father. Holy Spirit will reveal to us all things about our Father's heart. He is the Spirit of the living God. Holy Spirit lives inside of us. He is there to comfort us in our time of need. He stayed with me and wrapped His loving arms around me through all my hard times. Through every long night of tears, He was there. I could always feel the tangible presence of the Holy Spirit ministering to me. He is here to give us wisdom and knowledge of the things of the Kingdom. He shows us our Father's heart for us, giving us the strength and power to overcome in Him.

"But when the Father sends the Advocate as my representative - that is, the Holy Spirit - he will teach you everything and will remind you of everything I have told *you."* ~ John 14:26

Without the guidance of the Holy Spirit, we are really helpless in trying to make our own decisions in this world. I have found that if we give ourselves to the Lord and let the power of the Holy Spirit that lives in us be at work, there is much more peace. I also know He awakens us to the things we have done wrong in our lives so we can be free of them and be righteous in Christ Jesus. But most of all, I believe the Holy Spirit fills us so that we are so in love with Jesus that we lift Him up in everything we do in life. He fills us with the love and the presence of Jesus so that the world will know Him and see Him wherever we go.

I am forever thankful and forever grateful for my comforter and my best friend, Holy Spirit. Holy Spirit has taught me and shown me the beauty of who I am in Christ Jesus. It has changed everything in my life, even the way I think of myself. Now I see myself the way my Father sees me. I know I am everything beautiful and perfect to my Father.

"Don't you realize that your body is the temple of the Holy Spirit, who lives in you and was given to you by God? You do not belong to yourself, for God bought you with a high price. So you must honor God with your *body."* ~ 1 Corinthians 6:19-20

Father, we say come Holy Spirit come, fill this temple with the glory and the power of your Spirit! In Jesus name, Amen.

Perfect Love

"And God has given us his Spirit as proof that we live in him and he in us. Furthermore, we have seen with our own eyes and now testify that the Father sent his Son to be the Savior of the world. All who declare that Jesus is the Son of God have God living in them, and they live in God. We know how much God loves us, and we have put our trust in his love. God is love, and all who live in love live in God, and God lives in them. And as we live in God, our love grows more perfect. So we will not be afraid of the day of judgement, but we can face him with confidence because we live like Jesus here in this world. Such love has no fear, because perfect love expels all fear. If we are afraid, it is for fear of punishment, and this shows that we have not fully experienced his perfect love. We love each other because he loved us *first."* ~ 1 John 4:13-19

When I completely opened myself up to the Holy Spirit and allowed him to drop into my heart all the revelation from the Word of God, I became a new person. I have always known that God loved me, but this became more than just knowing. It became the truth of love. I felt so passionately loved and consumed by love that my issues didn't concern me like they did before. His perfect love spread through me like wild fire. I could literally feel the fire on my body, especially my head, hands, and feet. It didn't matter what came at me anymore. I even laughed at the issues I was having. My thoughts were, "What could anyone really do to me? I have a Father that is greater than any problem in this world." When we know our Father is in charge of all things in this world, we can relax and be more joyful. He wants us to have humor and joy in our lives, not worry

It was all about Jesus, not me. It was all about His perfection and His perfect love for me. When I came to Him and received His perfect love, He took all of my fears in exchange. I am now free to live in this world filled with the love of Jesus. The fire of His love warms my heart and flows out of me so I can love others. It is only with the love of Jesus that I or any of us can love an unloving world. It is only with the eyes of the heart of our Father that we can see others as He does. This is called Perfect Love, love that we as children of God carry inside of us to give to the world. There is no one who could ever take this love away from me or from you. It's time we all be a carrier of the love of Jesus. It is time that we let love flow out of us into our homes, cities, workplace, and nation, wherever the Lord wants to send us.

"And I am convinced that nothing can ever separate us from God's love. Neither death nor life, neither angels nor demons, neither our fears for today nor our worries about tomorrow - not even the powers of hell can separate us from God's love. No power in the sky above or in the earth below - indeed, nothing in all

creation will ever be able to separate us from the love of God that is revealed in Christ Jesus our *LORD.*"
~ Romans 8:38-39

When Things Didn't Go My Way

"*Trust* in the LORD with all your heart; do not depend on your own understanding. Seek his will in all you do, and he will show you which path to *take.*" ~ Proverbs 3:5-6

I went through so many years of praying for healing and restoration for my marriage, but things weren't going my way. I know God does not like divorce, and He wants families to be restored. I truly thought He wanted this for me and my family. I sought Him for answers. I prayed for miracles, but that particular miracle never came. God brought me the greatest miracle that I could have ever imagined, and that is a restored relationship with Jesus Christ and God the Father. There is no greater gift! God has promised me that He is restoring my life. Sometimes our idea of restoring is not the same as His, but He has been true to all of His promises!

He is the better judge of what is best for my life. He knows what will keep me safe and on the path that He has planned for me. I had to remind myself that God knows our hearts. This means God knows the heart of everyone involved.

So when things don't go my way, as they sometimes don't, I know there is always a good reason why. I trust that the Lord has a much better plan. I never stop trusting His way.

I realized that I needed to grow and mature in His love and wisdom. I have had a lot of growing up in the Lord to do over the past seven years. God has done a mighty work in me, and I expect it to continue without end.

I still don't know all the mysteries of God's plans, but I do know that God loves the family. He loves my family, and He loves me. He created us on this earth, so He could have a family. God wants families to live as He created them to live, to love one another as Christ Jesus loves us, to be together in harmony and unity. I have seen in the spirit, and I am waiting for the manifestation of what the Lord has shown me of the great and wonderful things the Lord has for my family. He is a Great and Mighty God!

Holy Spirit, I pray for the power of resurrection life to be given to all families to bring healing and total restoration. In Jesus Holy Name, Amen.

Wait On the Lord

"Wait patiently for the LORD. Be brave and courageous. Yes, wait patiently for the *LORD."*
~ Psalms 27:14

I read this scripture and asked the Lord, "How do I tell someone to be brave and courageous when they are going through hard times?" I remember a friend gave me a bracelet with this scripture on it when my husband left me in 2010. I wore it for a long time. She said it had helped her through her battle. I was in a battle, and I felt there was no way out. You may feel like you are in a battle like this too. But I am here to tell you, there is freedom! Hold on to the promises of God, and stay in the Word. For His Word is alive. He is alive! It is the breath of the living God. God is doing a work in you, and He wants you to be brave and trust the process. The more you trust in Him, the more you will embrace and love the process. God will renew you and refresh you during this time. He will heal you and use you to heal and reach out to others.

There are so many things that God will teach you during this time. Don't rush it! Rest in Him, yield to Him, He is always there to help. The path may seem long and winding, but trust me, if you are keeping your eyes on Jesus, you are winding up the mountain. Before you know it, you will find yourself standing on top of the mountain with Jesus, looking down at the valley you came out of.

"*I* waited patiently for the LORD to help me, and he turned to me and heard my *cry.*" ~ Psalms 40:1

"*I* say to myself, "*The* LORD is my inheritance; therefore, I will hope in *him!*" The LORD is good to those who depend on him, to those who search for him. So it is good to wait quietly for salvation from the *LORD.*" ~ Lamentations 3:24-26

He Knows the Beginning and the End

"I am the Alpha and the Omega - the beginning and the *end,"* says the LORD God. *"I* am the one who is, who always was, and who is still to come - the Almighty *One."* ~ Revelation 1:8

Jesus Christ is the King of Kings and the Lord of Lords. He is the One who is and always will be. He is my everlasting God, the One in whom I worship and love with all my heart and soul. Jesus is the only one who knows my end, just as He knew my beginning and everything I did in between.

Jesus is the Kingdom of this world. He came into this world so that we may have the Kingdom of God in our lives once again. As we receive Him in our hearts, the Kingdom of God comes down from Heaven. I am forever grateful to the King of Kings! He lives forever in my heart.

"Pray like this: Our Father in heaven, may your name be kept holy. May your Kingdom come soon. May your will be done on earth, as it is in *heaven."* ~ Matthew 6:9-10

I am also grateful for my parents who took me to church as a child to learn the Word of God so that a seed was planted early. I am thankful for having grandmothers that prayed for me and relatives, sister-in-law's, brother-in-law's, aunts, uncles, and friends who never gave up on me. Never stop praying for your loved ones.

Pray according to the Word of God, and he will fulfill His promises.

If you are experiencing an ending to something or someone in your life right now, let me just say your loving God will be with you. Holy Spirit will walk you through the valley of the shadow of darkness and bring you into the light. If you are facing any kind of fear or hesitation about your new beginning, remember He is already there, waiting to show you all the great and wonderful things He has planned for you. Keep this in mind, He is always with us. So even in our tomorrow, He is already there waiting on us, so we know the future can only be greater and greater.

"For I know the plans I have for *you,"* says the LORD. *"They* are plans for good and not for disaster, to give you a future and a *hope."* ~ Jeremiah 29:11

He Is My Everything

I remember back in 2013 when I first met Katie Souza. We were on the grounds where Patricia King's XP Ministries were going to be having the Big Tent Event. We had all met there to pray over the grounds. Katie was giving a word the Lord had given her, and she went around the group and asked everyone to give one word as to what Jesus meant to them. The word that came to me was "Everything!" Jesus was my everything. He had become everything in my life.

At one time in my life, I couldn't understand how someone could make church and religion their everything. How could you love anyone more than your own husband and children? Thank God I now understand the religious spirit that I had. I am so grateful to the Lord that I am not under the law or in bondage to it, but I am free to understand and experience true love through Christ Jesus, the One who fulfilled the law.

Our soul consists of the mind, will, and emotions. Our heart is influenced by both our spirit and our soul. When we come to Jesus, our spirits are saved, but our souls are still in the process of being transformed into the likeness of Jesus. I have found that at times this battle between the flesh and the spirit can be a daily struggle. My soul had been used to having its way for so long, it was not so willing to give in easily, but every battle I won gave me that much more victory! I could see myself overcoming the small battles, and soon the small battles gave me strength to overcome larger territory. By continuing to yield to the Holy Spirit and His ways, I was gaining the victory that comes in Christ Jesus!

A few years ago, I met this amazing lady named Dr. Aiko Hormann through the Healing Rooms. She is a research scientist who specializes in the human brain and artificial intelligence. One time, she came to speak about how God had placed within us three brains that control the body, mind, and emotions. Our head, the mind, gives commands to every part of the body, the heart, and our deepest gut.

She talked about how powerful our thoughts were and what they could do to our physical and emotional bodies. Her research showed that our thoughts carried more power activity than sound waves emitted from a local radio or television station. And as powerful as our thoughts are, words we receive or speak are even more powerful! This was an amazing revelation for me. I had spent most of my life hearing negative words. These words had played over and over in my thoughts like a movie for years. I knew about the power of words and was always aware of how words were affecting me, but I never realized how much power our thoughts had.

She explained that past hurts, sin, old memories, negative emotions, and un-forgiveness, all block the flow of the Holy Spirit in our lives. When we free ourselves of these things, the Holy Spirit can flow freely through us. Oh man, did God have a work to do in me! I was like one of those superhero Transformer toys my grandson plays with. God was about to do more than restore me, He was about to transform me into the one He created me to be.

I had no doubt in my mind, I was not going to hold on to anything that would block the flow of the Holy Spirit. When the Holy Spirit revealed things to me that needed healing, I let them go and gave them to the Lord, for He says to cast all your cares on Him. If thoughts came to me in the night that was of the past that needed to go, I would begin to worship the Lord in song. If I had to sing the same song over and over again for hours, I would. Healing comes when you worship the Lord in song.

"Have you never heard? Have you never understood? The LORD is the everlasting God, the Creator of all the earth. He never grows weak or weary. No one can measure the depths of his understanding. He gives power to the weak and strength to the powerless. Even youths will become weak and tired, and young men will fall in exhaustion. But those who trust in the LORD will find new strength. They will soar high on wings like eagles. They will run and not grow weary. They will walk and not *faint."* ~ Isaiah 40:28-31

My First and My Last

I love this quote I saw some time ago by an unknown author.

> Watch your thoughts; they become words.
> Watch your words; they become actions.
> Watch your actions; they become habits
> Watch your habits; they become character.
> Watch your character; it becomes your destiny.

We have all heard people say you are what you eat, and for the most part, that seems to be true. But what about what you watch on television, the type of music you listen to, the type of books you read, or places you go, etc.

I started out as young as grammar school watching a TV show about a vampire and the dark world of the supernatural. I remember hurrying home to see the show every day. My parents never said anything about it. No one ever realized there was any harm being done. It was a very popular show, and everyone watched it. That's one of the enemy's tactics, because everybody else is doing it or it's popular, we think its ok. I continued to watch these types of movies all through my life, never thinking they were doing me or my children or family any harm, until 2009.

When you watch these types of movies, you give the enemy access to your heart, your soul, and your life. What goes in will eventually come out, and God is always searching the heart of a man. He is looking to see if our heart is clean, or if it is filled with the ways of this fallen world. God says we are to be in this world but not to be of it. If He calls us to this way of life, sending Jesus to model it for us, we can all do it. God doesn't give us anything that He doesn't equip us to do.

"As a face is reflected in water, so the heart reflects the real person." ~ Proverbs 27:19

I had been praying for my family one day, breaking generational curses. That night I went to a wedding at our church with a girlfriend. I was perfectly healthy, but the minute I went to get out of the car at my house, I experienced this horrible pain in my chest. By the time I got inside my home, I could barely walk or breathe. I had to be taken to the emergency room. Everyone thought it was my heart, but I was diagnosed with pneumonia.

That same night I had a dream. I was in my car and my ex-husband came up to the window and said, "I like your cat." I looked and there was a black cat wrapped around my neck. I reached up and touched it. Realizing I didn't own a cat, I grabbed it from my neck and threw it to the ground. The Lord showed me that this was a demonic spirit that was trying to strangle me. It took me a while to recover in the physical, but I have been supernaturally healed from ever wanting to be a part of anything that is not of the supernatural Kingdom of God.

I thought that the movies I had been watching and the books I had been reading were innocent. I was so drawn to the supernatural. Now I understand that it was natural for me to be drawn to it, for I am a spirit being. It's just that I had been drawn into the counterfeit. There were generational curses in our family that needed to be broken also.

My friends, I am here to tell you, we have to be aware of what goes into our eye gates, for it is the window to our souls. We must set our eyes on the things of God and not be drawn in by the ruler of this world!

"*Since* you have been raised to new life with Christ, set your sights on the realities of heaven, where Christ sits in the place of honor at *God's* right hand. Think about the things of heaven, not the things of *earth.*" ~ Colossians 3:1-2

We become like the things we focus on and continue to behold. That's why it's important to focus on the good, the beautiful, and the positive things in life, and I behold the King of Kings! He is my first and my last. He is the one I wake up to in the morning and the one I go to bed with in the evening. Jesus' love has filled my heart, and that is who I am today.

"And now, dear brothers and sisters, one final thing. Fix your thoughts on what is true, and honorable, and right, and pure, and lovely, and admirable. Think about things that are excellent and worthy of *praise."*
~ Philippians 4:8

"Study this Book of Instruction continually. Meditate on it day and night so you will be sure to obey everything written in it. Only then will you prosper and succeed in all you *do."* ~ Joshua 1:8

"Guard your heart above all else, for it determines the course of your *life."* ~ Proverbs 4:23

Entrusting My Life to Him

"But Moses told the people, *"Don't* be afraid. Just stand still and watch the LORD rescue you today. The Egyptians you see today will never be seen again. The LORD himself will fight for you. Just stay calm." ~ Exodus 14:13-14

Everyone knows the story of how God used Moses to lead His people out of Egypt and out of the bondage of slavery. After God sent all the plagues, Pharaoh let God's people go. So Moses gathered all the people and led them into the wilderness. God watched over them the whole time they were there. He gave them fire by night so they could see and to keep them warm. They had a cloud by day to protect them from the heat, and He led the way. He fed them food from heaven and water from the rocks. Their shoes never wore out. They left Egypt totally and completely healed and full of wealth. God just poured His love all over them. These were people who had been so beaten down for generations, but despite all of His amazing love, all they did was complain.

When I read that story back in 2010, my heart wept for Our Father and how He must have felt, loving His children so much and yet they be so unloving. For forty years He continued to give to them, and they continued to complain. It's like they would be excited when the miracles came, then forget the very next day.

Then I got to thinking about my own life and how I had been in bondage for forty years. And when I say bondage, I am talking about bondage to the plans of the enemy. When you are not walking with Jesus, you are walking with the ruler of this world. You are agreeing with His plans for your life. I saw myself a lot like those people. I had so much to be thankful for in my life, but at the same time I was complaining about my situations. Whether they were my choice or not, how I reacted to them was. I have a choice on how I respond to the situations in my life, and I also take full responsibility for the decisions I make.

It was the enemy's plan from the very beginning to destroy our relationships and our lives. He will not ever give up. He is delusional. He knows he has lost the battle, but he wants to take as many of God's children with Him as possible, and he is going to do it at any cost. That's why we are to always be ready for battle. We are warriors in the army of God.

"The serpent was the shrewdest of all the wild animals the LORD God had made. One day he asked the woman, "Did God really say you must not eat the fruit from any of the trees in the garden?" ~ Genesis 3:1

Satan first attacks our relationship with God, wanting us to doubt what we already have in Christ Jesus. Then he starts working on the couples, trying to get one or both of them to make wrong choices. That really tears a family apart, because this is where the fighting begins. Then, satan gets us to blame each other for our mistakes, just like Adam pointed the finger at Eve in the garden. This tactic works for him every time. Satan uses negative thoughts, unforgiveness, bitterness, and selfishness to divide and destroy until there is nothing left of what God put together. It's happening in so many marriages and relationships. It happened to mine. Thank God for those who had eyes to see, those who forgave, and received restoration.

All the plans of the enemy have been destroyed. They were destroyed at the cross. We have won victory over every one of them. God's children who recognize who they are in Him are great and mighty warriors. The enemy is afraid of the power that is in the unit of a Godly marriage and a Godly family.

"Stay alert! Watch out for your great enemy, the devil. He prowls around like a roaring lion, looking for someone to *devour."* ~ 1 Peter 5:8

"But you belong to God, my dear children. You have already won a victory over those people, because the Spirit who lives in you is greater than the spirit who lives in the *world."* ~ 1 John 4:4

Just as Moses heard God's voice and trusted Him to lead the people out of bondage, I am forever grateful that I heard the voice of God calling, and I finally came out of the wilderness. I am forever grateful for His amazing grace because I now live a life of such freedom. Freedom to love, freedom to receive love, and freedom to give love. I put all my trust in my God, for He is loving and merciful. He does great and mighty things for us all the time. There is no one greater than our God. Put all your trust in Him, for He has great and mighty plans for each and every one of us.

Father, I pray today for broken relationships, for hearts that have been broken and crushed. I pray that you would give them peace of mind in their hearts and fill them with hope to see their relationships restored as they are restored in you. Set their hearts afire with love and passion, a fresh new love for you and each other. May their lives be a testimony of the Power and the Glory of the Name of Christ Jesus! In Jesus Holy Name, Amen.

My Ultimate Peace

"*And* let the peace that comes from Christ rule in your hearts. For as members of one body you are called to live in peace. And always be *thankful*" ~ Collossians 3:15

"*Don't* worry about anything; instead pray about everything. Tell God what you need, and thank him for all he has done. Then you will experience *God's* peace, which exceeds anything we can understand. His peace will guard your heart and minds as you live in Christ *Jesus.*" ~ Philippians 4:6-7

For a child is born to us, a son is given to us. The government will rest on his shoulders. And he will be called: Wonderful Counselor, Mighty God, Everlasting Father, Prince of Peace. ~ Isaiah 9:6

"*For* Christ himself has brought peace to us. He united Jews and Gentiles into one people when, in his own body on the cross, he broke down the wall of hostility that separated us. He did this by ending the system of law with its commandments and regulations. He made peace between Jews and Gentiles by creating in himself one new people from the two groups. Together as one body, Christ reconciled both groups to God by means of his death on the cross, and our hostility toward each other was put to *death.*" ~ Ephesians 2:14-16

God said a child would be born to us. God said His Son would be given to us, and He is the Prince of Peace. God says peace is a person, and in order for you and me to live at peace with ourselves or anyone else, we must be at peace with the person of Jesus Christ. When you have His peace, you can begin to deal with all the other issues this life throws at you. You must start with you and Jesus! Oneness with Jesus is the secret. I have found that the closer I get to Him, the more at peace my heart becomes. Jesus is the secret that bridges the gap between peace and anyone or situation that may be troubling you. Imagine Him always standing between you and that situation.

I have had many dreams and visions of being with Jesus, and I always find peace in His presence. I recall a dream where I looked to be in the eye of a tornado, but Jesus was there. I had no fear, only peace. When things of this world are going crazy and spinning out of control, He will be your peace. I find myself resting on His chest all the time and receiving His peace. God's peace is so different than anything in this world. It goes to a place deep inside and gives rest and comfort to our hearts and minds.

I am forever grateful to the Wonderful Counselor, Mighty God, Everlasting Father, and the Prince of Peace.

Father, I pray that you bring peace to the hearts of all your loved ones. Break down walls that separate us, and lead us on the path of righteousness for your namesake. In Jesus Holy Name, Amen.

Meet the Author

Sheila Waits is a passionate lover of Jesus Christ, and a dedicated intercessor for XP Ministry. She has a passion to see the fire and glory of God move throughout the Body of Christ, to see God's people be touched by the power of the Holy Spirit, and a heart to see the Body of Christ living in complete and total freedom in Jesus.

Sheila is a mother of three grown children and three beautiful grandchildren. She lives in Phoenix, Arizona.

Send all prayer requests and testimonies to
sheilawaits.heart2heal@gmail.com

If *"Freedom in Christ"* has blessed you in any way, please consider leaving a review to help me spread this message of triumph and healing.

1. Go to www.amazon.com
2. Search for "Freedom in Christ" by Sheila Waits.
3. Scroll to the bottom and click on "Write a Customer Review"
4. Rate the book (out of 5 stars) and write your review

Please Note: Before you can post a review, you need to have an Amazon.com account that has successfully been charged for the purchase of a physical or digital item. Free digital downloads don't qualify. You don't need to have purchased the product you're reviewing. There's a 48-hour waiting period after your first physical order has been completely shipped, or your digital item has been purchased, before you'll be able to submit your review. Thank you in advance for your positive review.

Made in the USA
San Bernardino, CA
06 February 2017